TIME
for
SUCCESS

*A Goal Getter's
Strategy*

TIME
for
SUCCESS

A Goal Getter's Strategy

Alec Mackenzie

McGraw-Hill, Inc.

New York   St. Louis   San Francisco   Auckland   Bogotá   Caracas
Hamburg   Lisbon   London   Madrid   Mexico   Milan   Montreal
New Delhi   Paris   San Juan   São Paulo   Singapore
Sydney   Tokyo   Toronto

1 2 3 4 5 6 7 8 9 0 FGR/FGR 8 9 2 1 0 9

ISBN 0-07-044653-9 {HC}
ISBN 0-07-044656-3 {PBK}

Library of Congress Cataloging-in-Publication Data

Mackenzie, Alec.
  Time for success.
  Includes index.
  1. Success in business. I. Title.
HF5386.M225 1989   650.1   88-37285
ISBN 0-07-044653-9 (hc)
ISBN 0-07-044656-3 (pbk)

Book design by Eve L. Kirch

To Gay, without whose patience, understanding, gentle reminders, and perseverance this book would never have been written.

CONTENTS

INTRODUCTION

Do you remember how you felt when you hit your first home run? Or when you served your first perfect soufflé? Or the day your boss quietly commented, "Great work"? Those were moments of success when you knew a job had been well done or a new level of expertise had been reached.

All of us like to feel good about ourselves. We would be glad to experience these kinds of successes more often. Conversely, we do not enjoy the sense of failure. We particularly do not enjoy being measured against other people and found wanting. Yet we don't all have the same capabilities, nor are we all performing under identical circumstances. What, then, can we do to maintain our self-esteem and ensure that we frequently experience success?

What is this thing called success? Surely it varies from person to person? For a runner or a mountaineer success may mean physical achievement, or it may mean mental discipline or the conquest of fear. For a student struggling with a math problem, it may be the moment of breakthrough to the solution. For the computer salesperson it may be the first glance at the upward curve of the graph on the monthly chart. For a mother it may be the first time her shy son is confident enough to spend the night away from home. Why, when success is so dear to us, is it so difficult to manage? Every New Year's Day, thousands resolve to seek success in their personal and professional lives. They may write exhaustive lists of resolutions or goals, which in a day or two are for the most part broken or discarded.

This book will guide you step-by-step through a consideration of the nature of success, the way we set goals for ourselves to ensure success, and, in particular, the way we handle that precious commodity—time—without which the achievement of any goal is impossible. It shows you the essential relationships among goals, time, and success in life.

Expect some surprises. You may change your mind about what constitutes success. You may decide that people you once thought successful do not qualify after all. You will discover that success does not have as much to do with status or capabilities as you believed. You will almost certainly recognize yourself as a candidate for success.

You will come to realize the importance of goals, properly used, in the achievement of success. You will be helped to monitor your progress toward success by the implementation of interim checkpoints on the way. Each small success you experience will make the next step easier and the probability of ultimate success greater.

This book is a tool that will help you achieve success in every aspect of your life.

CHAPTER

What Is Success?

GETTING YOUR ACT TOGETHER

Do you know people who always do what they say they will? Exactly? And on time? They always seem to know where they're going and why, and they have a plan for how they're going to get there. They work hard, enjoy what they do, and make a real contribution to the organization. When you ask them to do something, they don't say "maybe." They say "yes" or "no." If they say "no," you can be sure they have a good reason why they can't do it or shouldn't do it. If they say "yes," you can depend on them to get it done. They'll always ask when it's needed, because that's the key to whether or not they can complete the project on time. They always deliver. We say that such people "have their act together." It's one of the highest compliments we pay. It's a badge of success. I've known a few people like this, and I'd like to tell you about them.

One, a researcher-writer-editor, is raising two children and works part-time to allow her husband, herself, and her family to follow their varied interests, ranging from extensive gardening and mountain climbing in the summer to skiing in the winter. When you ask her to do something, she enquires into the purpose, details, and deadline. Then she'll say something like this: "I'll work it out in the light of my other priorities; then I'll come back and tell you how long it will take, and I'll recommend a way of meeting the deadline without jeopardizing other projects. If that's satisfactory, I'll proceed." She thinks things through, and she anticipates how long tasks will take and what could go wrong. She keeps her personal and business goals clear and never lets one interfere with the other. Yes, she has her act together. She has been successful in most everything she's tackled.

Another friend has written, lectured, and consulted extensively on the topics of goal setting and objectives achievement. He manages to have time for involvement in many activities, such as the National Speakers' Association, and he accomplishes more than anyone I know. He's always clear on his objectives, both personal and business; he concentrates his efforts on making them happen. He is well known for his writing on objectives, particularly his book *Getting Your Act Together.** When I first saw the title, my reaction was, "He's just the one to write that book." In it he says:

> Getting your act together is not primarily a function of intelligence, financial resources, environment, associates, position, or any of the other factors usually associated with success, although any of these factors can play a part in success. Getting your act together is, very simply, identifying what you want to do, knowing how to do it, and then doing it: in other words, setting and achieving goals.

---

*George Morrissey, *Getting Your Act Together*, Wiley, New York, 1980.

CHANGING VALUES AND SUCCESS

In the late 1970s the competing values of home and family began to modify the long-held image of success in business. Previously, corporate promotions that involved relocating families had not been questioned, much less rejected. The personal upheaval was regarded as the price of success, the price for moving up in the organization. However, values were changing. When many of my friends in Chappaqua, New York, worked for IBM, they said, only half-jokingly, that "IBM" meant "I've Been Moved." One of them told me that the problem of short tenure in the same job was given attention after a survey revealed the average tenure in the same job was nine months. The ready acceptance of tying promotions to transfers began to change. Transfers with pay raises were refused by managers who decided their family interests came first. Many fast-track executives took themselves out of the fast lane when their professional goals clashed with their personal goals.

Should such decisions block managers from "successful" careers? Is it right to consider that someone is less successful simply because he or she passed up a promotion and a salary increase in favor of family interests? The reaction in many corporate headquarters was disbelief. But the number of rejections continued to increase until corporations realized the refusals were not a passing phenomenon. Today many corporate policies have been modified to accommodate those who are qualified for promotion but who prefer not to move. When two-career families are moved, corporate assistance in placing spouses in positions comparable to their former employment is increasingly common, which indicates that corporations are recognizing the importance of family values.

The Naisbitt Group predicts continuing trends in this direction as the baby boomers reach 40 years of age.* Oriented

---

*"Out of Time," *The American Way,* December 1987.

toward future rather than present thinking, baby boomers will be less materialistic in outlook, less consumption-driven, and therefore less inclined to work harder to earn more money. They will place a higher value on relationships, especially among family members, and their attention will be turned more toward quality-of-life issues.

NEW ROLES AFFECT CONCEPTS OF SUCCESS

Today's concepts of "goals" and "success" are quite different from those of ten years ago. The parents of today's baby boomers knew exactly what their goals were: Men had jobs and provided for wives and children; women cared for home and family and sometimes worked as nurses or teachers. But for baby boomers, and for their children, growing up to be just like their parents is no longer considered enough. The civil rights movement, the women's rights movement, and the new information-age economy have opened up opportunities and changed many lifestyles.

New roles have been created and new family patterns have been established. It is not unusual for a woman to head a corporation; a male single parent may care for a preschool child. You will find families in which the father of two children works as an overburdened doctor, the mother as a busy lawyer. In some households the woman may commute to work daily, while the father stays at home to rear the children; that father may work part-time on a night shift. Few models for these situations and roles existed in the previous generation, so few people can offer help in setting guidelines for these new lifestyles.

Breaking new ground is risky business, and self-doubt is a constant problem when you're not sure how to get where you are going. In 1960, 19 percent of all women, married and unmarried, with preschool children were in the labor force. In 1986, that figure was a startling 52 percent. For many of these women, not rearing their children the way their mothers did is extremely distressing. And they are haunted by a nagging question: Is where I'm going where I'll want to be?

Men and women alike strive for professional success. Yet they aren't even sure how to define "success." They do have a sense of urgency about the need to go out there and "do something," but they don't have well-formulated goals. Many are beginning to question whether professional success must preclude personal success, personal happiness. They seek well-rounded lives.

For many who have demanding jobs, a primary goal is having interests outside the job and adequate time to pursue them. But "adequate time" to pursue outside interests is in short supply. Indeed, the time scarcity in the United States is being intensified by the growing demands for consumer products and the longer working hours required to afford them. A recent study showed that leisure time has decreased from twenty-six to sixteen hours per week. The Naisbitt Group found that western Europeans who maintain a traditional view of work and leisure and are not as consumption-driven as Americans enjoy two to three times as much vacation time. So the goal of well-rounded lives is proving elusive. No wonder so many people are feeling frustrated with the difficulty in achieving success both at work and at home.

SUCCESS IS SELDOM WHAT IT SEEMS

The outward appearance of success can often be misleading. Those who "made it to the top" often turn out to be there only in a transitory sense. A cab driver picked me up at a hotel in a wealthy suburb of Chicago. I asked him if he'd always driven a taxi. It turned out he'd owned a gas station in that suburb but had gone out of business because his customers didn't pay their bills. I asked how that could happen in such a community. He replied: "Easy. Most of the families here are living beyond their incomes. They want the address to impress people for business reasons, but they can't pay their bills. Many of the homes we're passing have no furniture upstairs. They're sleeping on mattresses on the floors."

Today, increasing numbers of "successes" are pleading guilty to charges of perjury and violations of ethics, being imprisoned for embezzlement, and even committing suicide. Star athletes confess to being drug addicts or steroid users, politicians are being exposed for unprincipled behavior, and televangelists are being defrocked. We can easily conclude that success is seldom what it seems.

REAL SUCCESS IS DOING YOUR BEST

So what does one do? Let's begin by redefining "success." If getting to the top is *not* necessarily a definition of success, what is? Success is "doing your best." In school, this means that a "C" student who is doing his or her best is more successful than an "A" student who is not. Simple and clear. In business, in personal affairs, in family matters, in school—in all situations the person who is performing close to potential is more successful than the person who is not.

I was having dinner with a good friend at a major sales convention. He complained that every time he came to this particular convention he ran into salespeople who were doing a lot better than he was and it made him feel like a failure. "I have the same hours in the day as they do," he explained. "I'm good at what I do. I know the business upside down, and I know how to sell. And I'm as smart as they are. I just can't understand how they can be doing so much better." We talked about the folly of measuring oneself against the world and about the sense of failure and permanent frustration such a comparison is bound to create. Obviously, no two salespeople in the world are in exactly the same situation, with exactly the same products to sell and the same prospects with the same needs. I reminded him of the outstanding reputation he'd achieved within his own company. The president had told me my friend was the finest person he'd ever hired. His sales were excellent; he was very well off; he had a remarkable family, lived in a beautiful home, enjoyed many friends, and was the envy of most who knew him. The stress of competition, however, and the feeling of comparative failure had led him to take work home and to work longer hours than he really wanted to, which was costing him time with his family. After a while my friend said quietly: "You know, it isn't easy to accept, because I'm a natural competitor. But I think you're right. I should be measuring my performance against my own potential and be satisfied when I know I've done my best."

I was sitting beside a teacher from a college in the midwest who was telling me about an unusual success story. A "C" student had just graduated "with highest honors." The reason? In the major project of her senior year, she had done the best work ever seen in the department. She was deemed the student in that department most likely to succeed and was therefore worthy of the highest honors the department could bestow. We can assume that this student was striving hard and doing her best to maintain her "C" average. In that category alone she would therefore be more successful than many of the "A" students who were neither trying hard nor doing their best.

The fact that this student outperformed all others with higher grades when it came to the special project points to the doubtful techniques being used in many school systems to select the "gifted and talented" students for enrichment experiences. For example, I'm currently involved in teaching leadership skills, such as listening and goal setting, to young people. A fifth-grade student whose "C" average had prevented her from ever being selected for the enrichment programs scored highest in her class on the leadership skills audit. Teachers involved in the school's "gifted and talented" programs are questioning whether the policy of selecting students with the highest grades should be reexamined. These teachers seek a redefinition of "success" that would consider the individual's personal commitment to achievement and to doing one's best. The present system, which is increasingly felt to be unsatisfactory, measures students solely against a predetermined grade scale.

WHEN LOSING IS REALLY WINNING

A recent event solidified my conviction that success should be defined as doing your best. A gold medalist in Olympic Greco-Roman wrestling lives in a neighboring town. Naturally, I've taken more than a casual interest in his success. He had to overcome several handicaps to achieve his remarkable victory: He had contracted Hodgkin's disease, and he came from a family unable to provide him with the specialized training usually mandated for Olympic hopefuls. However, his life's motto was "Do your best." He did his best, and his gold medal testifies that his best was better than anyone else's in that Olympic competition. Unfortunately, his cancer recurred. He persevered in his fight against the disease and began training for the next Olympics. When he was interviewed by the press about his ambitions for the coming competition, reporters pressed him about how he would view not winning the gold medal, if that should be the case. "My target is not to win," he said, "but to show by the sweat of my brow and the gleam in my eye that I've done my best. If doing my best is good enough to win, so be it. If it is not, so be that. Doing my best is winning for me." No one has ever suggested a better definition for success. And never was so clear a definition more needed. Without such a definition we are crowning false heroes, bestowing unearned honors, and increasing the burden of failure when much of failure is really success. Since all of us can do our best if we try, real success is in the trying. In a Dale Carnegie course I took many years ago, I saw my first example of this different kind of success. It was an award for "the most improved speaker" in the course. Each week that award always drew the greatest applause, and well it should.

THE MOST SUCCESSFUL FAILURE I'VE KNOWN

A salesman I met recently might well have been the product of a school system that placed a strong emphasis on competitive grades. He is a perfect example of the need for a better definition of success. Not yet 30 years old, he has won practically every award his company offers in terms of sales records for his years of service. Curiously, his last and highest award was unexciting, he said, because he knew all along that he would win it and even when he would do so. He was obviously coasting on a comfortable course, accepting what his company thought were high goals as mere routine challenges. I asked him what his sales goal for the next year was. He said it was to keep on the same path he'd been on because it had been successful. "Is coasting your idea of success?" I asked him. "Well, my record is pretty good," he countered modestly. "Measured against what?" I queried. "Are you measuring yourself against the sales of others or against the best you are capable of doing yourself?" He thought a moment; then he replied, "Well, you're always measured against others, I guess."

We discussed the problem of defining success by comparison with others. After all, the best of a number of companies going into bankruptcy will still be going broke, and the best of a poor lot of salespeople may still be far below his or her potential. Having become bored with his work, the award-winning salesman was considering quitting his job and finding something that would be more challenging. He had failed to see that his lack of motivation was primarily due to his own failure to set demanding goals. He reassessed his situation and set more demanding goals; this year, his sales figure was twice that of last year. For the first time in years he feels motivated. He now finds his work stimulating, challenging, and rewarding.

MAKE A FRIEND OF FAILURE

We are not usually congratulated for our failures. We quickly learn at home, at school, and, later, at work that failure is to be deplored and avoided. We grow up ashamed of failure, and the most successful people become very good at concealing it. How many parents take the view that an "F" on a report card is a golden opportunity to work together with their child, to overcome a difficulty? Do we regard a serious family misunderstanding as the starting point for a new successful relationship? When an office employee destroys a computer disc full of information, does the boss welcome the mistake as evidence that the employee will one day become a valuable resource because the worker has experienced failure early in his or her career?

Henry Ford II provided us with such a positive view of failure. One of his executives pursued an expenditure of $20 million that resulted in total failure. Approaching Henry, the executive said he presumed his career at Ford was over. "Nothing of the kind," said Henry. "We've spent too much educating you to even dream of losing you."

There is no doubt that our attitude toward failure conditions our successes and that we can learn more about how to succeed by taking an analytical look at why we fail. Salespeople have the most positive attitude toward failure. They experience it on a regular basis if they view a rejection by a prospect as a failure. However, the best salespeople don't view rejection as failure at all. They view it as a necessary part of the sales game. A friend told me: "The sooner I get nine rejections, the sooner I make the sale. So the faster they come, the better!"

My study of leadership has led to countless examples of world successes who suffered great failures before they succeeded. Winston Churchill's school record was so poor that his parents consigned him to the military—the Siberia of its day in England. Wernher von Braun failed his first course in mathematics, but he was strong enough to return to the subject, study it fiercely, and eventually master it.

Friends of mine in the training profession are of one mind in counseling against hiring an employee who can't recall ever making a really big mistake. If the person is not telling the truth, that's serious. But if he or she *is* telling the truth, the person is a very high risk. Such people have never had the chance to demonstrate their ability to recover from failure. No one wants to provide them with the first such opportunity.

DOING YOUR BEST DOESN'T COME NATURALLY

My work with top-producing salespeople has provided an excellent arena for testing how human nature works in terms of doing one's best. The top 25 of a company's 3000 salespeople met with me to discuss how they could improve their own records. I asked if they felt they had reached their outstanding sales levels primarily because of managing well or in spite of managing poorly. Immediately, the members of the group began reminding each other of their obvious disorganization, lack of planning, inability to remember critical things and to track progress, missed deadlines, and constant crises that should have been avoided. One salesperson was reminded that he had misplaced an application for a million-dollar policy that had never been found! Overall, the consensus was that they had reached their present positions in spite of not managing well. In addition, they admitted that they were bored and no longer found their jobs challenging. Few of them were setting difficult goals and sensing the daily enthusiasm that comes from setting and achieving demanding targets.

These people were the "success" stories of their company; they had been honored for their "outstanding" accomplishments. Since, by their own admission, not one of them was doing his or her best, each now realized that personal success was in doubt: They were failures when measured against their own potential. Ah yes, "successful failures." A new term, but descriptive.

Without question, there were many dozens—if not hundreds—of more successful salespeople at lower levels in that organization! People with a lot less ability were working a lot harder to achieve goals that were a lot more demanding for them. Those who came closer to fulfilling their potential than did these "top" 25 were more successful by my definition.

MAKE SUCCESS YOUR GOAL

Almost all successful people attribute their success, at least in part, to goals. If success is defined as the progressive realization of goals, then goals are a prerequisite to success. Also, if we add that doing our best is succeeding and that without goals we will not be motivated to do our best, once again we see that goals are imperative to success.

I use the term *goal getter* to characterize a successful person. "Goal getter" combines in one term the ideas of both setting goals and achieving them. It combines the two secrets of success: Setting your sights high and pursuing your goals systematically. So we turn in Chapter 2 to goals—why people resist their use and, most important, how to set them to ensure success.

CHAPTER

Setting Goals for Success

How many times have you said: "I've always dreamed of . . . ," or "I wish I could . . .," or "Someday I'm going to . . . ," or perhaps on New Year's Eve, "Next year I'm really going to . . ."? On reflection we know what happens to most of our dreams, our wishes, our good intentions, and, yes, our New Year's resolutions. Few of them ever come to fruition. Our predicament is dramatized in the saying "The road to hell is paved with good intentions." Only a few days into this year two newscasters joked about having already broken their New Year's resolutions. The failures we've experienced in achieving our hopes and dreams, our wishes and intentions, have two common causes: lack of time (which we will consider in the next chapter) and lack of sound goals. For hopes and dreams to be transformed into reality, they must be cast in terms of valid goals. Certain steps are essential for that to happen. In this chapter we will explore the need to develop goals and will establish their importance as a basis for success. We'll identify the steps that need to be taken to ensure that our goals are valid and explain how to target those goals for success at work and at home.

NEED FOR GOALS NOT NEW

We can all recall having dealings with someone who was obviously bored and frustrated by his or her job. A friend of mine walked into the local newspaper office to place an advertisement but was unable to get the clerk's attention. The clerk was talking on the phone, filing her nails, and chewing gum. My friend waited, patiently at first; as the phone conversation dragged on, her impatience grew. It was clear from the way the clerk ignored a prospective customer that she felt no commitment to her job and did not have the professionalism to conceal it. Here was a clear example of a young woman who had not been encouraged to develop goals for the part of her job that related to customer service. It is probable that she had no well-thought-out goals for the rest of her job either.

Do you remember our "most successful failure" in Chapter 1? He was bored and unmotivated, though most perceived him to be a success. By his company's standards, he was indeed a success. Only when he measured his performance against his potential did he see his failure. Demanding goals transformed his outlook and his sales performance doubled. For the first time in his life he saw the need for demanding goals. He also discovered that demanding goals can be very exciting and highly motivating.

THE SHIP WITHOUT A HARBOR

Our "most successful failure" learned for himself through trial and error what Seneca, the Roman writer, taught 2000 years ago. Seneca referred to the ship without a harbor, for which no wind can be the right one. The wisdom of his comment can be seen in its applicability to anyone without a goal. For such a person, no decision can be right, except by chance.

Indeed, why *are* goals necessary? Don't most of us get along pretty well without them? If getting along "pretty well" means that things could be worse, each of us would, of course, answer "yes." "But," you persist, "why should I worry about goals if I'm pretty well satisfied with things the way they are?" It's easy to be satisfied if you've never set goals. It's easy to say you're doing fine when you don't know where you're going. You can always say that any destination you arrive at is okay.

I was reminded of this not long ago at a major convention. I was about to give the keynote address on time management. By chance, I encountered an older gentleman whose chest was bedecked with ribbons indicating various local and regional offices he'd held in the organization. By way of making conversation, I asked if he was planning to attend the keynote session. "No," he responded, "I don't pay too much attention to those things." Since almost everyone attends the keynote sessions at these conventions, my curiosity was aroused. I mentioned that the topic was time management and I asked him if he ever needed more time. "Not really," he allowed. "I've pretty much gotten where I wanted to go, more or less, most of the time." My thoughts have gone back to that gentleman many times. Wasn't he really saying that wherever he happened to wind up was okay?

Some time later I was talking with my friend, Dick Brunsman, a leading salesman in the insurance industry. Dick had participated in my time-management study group sponsored by the Million Dollar Round Table. He'd increased his income ten times in the ten years following the study. He attributed this outstanding record to improved time control. After returning from a lecture tour, Dick said: "Guess what I've just learned! I've been puzzled over why some agents just aren't interested in time management. Now I know why. They don't

have any goals." Dick described these people with no goals
as being mired in the status quo. This brought to mind the
gentleman at the convention. He wasn't going anywhere, except wherever he chanced to wind up. Furthermore, I rea-
soned, he couldn't fail. Without goals, how *could* he fail? Yes,
he was getting by. His life was comfortable. He was satisfied.
Why should he want to change anything? Complacent, and
perhaps smug, he would never know the extent of his failure.
He would never test his potential performance. Whatever the
status quo happened to be was okay with him.

WHY WE RESIST SETTING GOALS

Each of us has probably forgotten or lost sight of some of
the goals we have set along the way. For most of us, simply
trying to set goals is not as easy as it sounds. Many of us resist
setting goals for a number of reasons. Take the experience of
a friend whose superior at work appointed him to represent
the company on the United Fund Drive Committee for the
community. At the first meeting he found himself chairing
the small-business division that his boss had chaired the previous year. The committee chairman was making the rounds
of the attendees and assigning quotas. When my friend's turn
came, the chairman announced: "We've set a goal of $50,000
for the small-business division. You have fifty small businesses
to contact, so that's an average of only $1000 from each one."
My friend's heart beat faster. The quota was a complete surprise to him, and he resented being informed in this way. He
didn't want to look like a piker, but asking for money, even
for a good cause, was not exactly his cup of tea. He'd never
done it before and wouldn't be doing it now if his boss hadn't
volunteered his services. It sounded like a huge sum of money.
And what if he failed? There were a lot of influential people
sitting around the table who probably would have no difficulty
raising their quotas.

Fear of failure causes almost everyone to resist setting goals. In addition, my friend's resistance was further intensified since he had not participated in setting the goal he was now committed to.

In contrast, suppose your boss announces a new program of goal setting and says it's time to plan for next year. You are asked to submit your suggested goals within a week. This gives you plenty of time to consult with your team and to formulate your suggestions for goals for the coming year. Still, you feel uncomfortable having to commit to a course of action so far in advance. You prize your independence and see the acceptance of goals as infringing on your freedom to act independently. Perhaps you aren't really sure how to set goals and don't really appreciate their benefits. If you feel you've done quite well without them, why are they necessary?

HOW GOALS MOTIVATE

As I've thought about goals, one thing has become increasingly clear. They motivate. Some time ago I wondered why I wasn't making the marketing calls I knew I should be making for my company. There wasn't a lack of prospects; my assistants had been doing a good job of developing them. I didn't lack confidence in the company's products and services. Of course, I did have call reluctance; no one wants to be rejected, and salespeople can easily feel rejected when someone isn't interested in what they're selling. I finally realized that I'd lost sight of my sales goals. By losing sight of them, I really was operating without them. My days were being driven not by my real priorities but by an endless stream of interruptions, staff requests, and tasks I found more pleasing than sales calls. A few articles needed to be written, a task I enjoy. A final book review was due, and an exciting project of teaching leadership skills to young people had been suggested. My desk was full of things that attracted my attention every day. My goals for making sales calls had become lost in the shuffle of more exciting tasks.

With a red felt-tip pen, I wrote down on a flip chart the top prospects for sales calls. I put the amounts of the prospective orders beside the names and added a few columns to track my progress in making these calls. I placed the flip chart on an easel and positioned it so that it confronted me when I entered my office and when I was at my desk. By keeping the chart visible in this manner, I was reminded of the important calls every time I glanced at the chart. It worked wonders. As a call was completed, I either entered the amount of the sale or crossed it off as a "no sale." My energy was focused on that chart as I watched the monthly goal gradually being approached. Whenever I was talking on a nonsales call, the chart in front of me was a visible reminder that the call I was on was not moving me toward my goals. What a reminder that was! I had gone from a condition of having practically no goals, since they hadn't been visible, to having goals that were the focal point of all office activity. Surprisingly, there was even satisfaction in crossing out the "no sales." It cleared the chart of nonproductive prospects, which I then worked at replacing with more productive ones. This permitted me to measure my success at regular intervals, which, in turn, provided a sense of satisfaction and a desire to improve.

Yes, goals *do* motivate, provided you keep them visible. Who will forget the story of the football back who momentarily lost sight of *his* goal and scored a touchdown—that's right—for the *other* team!

Goals motivate because they provide benchmarks of success. They enable us to track our progress and to know how well we are doing at any point in time. Goals motivate in other ways as well. Think for a moment of the last time you were assigned a task either at work or perhaps in a volunteer organization. The person assigning the task took time to explain the big picture: the background of the task, why it was important, and the part it played in the larger organizational framework. This background motivated you to do a better job, since you understood that your task was contributing to something bigger. It gave you a feeling of importance, and you were better able to cope with unexpected problems as they arose. Your commitment to the task was enhanced by an understanding and appreciation of your own contribution. Your efforts were given purpose and direction. Appreciating your own role in the larger effort enhanced your sense of well-being and self-confidence as well. Knowing that your work would produce beneficial and worthwhile results raised your level of expectation. A task that is unexplained and therefore not understood becomes uninteresting and unrewarding. It will be done less well as a result.

THE GENIUS OF MEASUREMENT

The flip chart in my office showed me another advantage in keeping goals visible. I already knew that keeping goals visible enhances the likelihood of accomplishing them. After all, you can't do what you can't remember. But the motivational impact of visible goals was something I had overlooked. Rewards are a known motivator. But rewards too long deferred tend to lose their impact. By listing targeted sales for the month, I could tell how much closer to my monthly goal each sale brought me. Each sale became a success, a checkpoint or benchmark bringing me that much closer to my goal for the month. Each measurement, in effect, becomes a motivator. If the sales figure at the end of the first week fell short of the targeted figure, I was immediately motivated to take the action needed to make up for that deficit. Alternatively, if the sales exceeded the target, a feeling of exhilaration resulted. Sometimes a new and higher target was warranted. After sensing this feeling many times, and discussing it with others, I became convinced that the genius of measuring performance against demanding goals is its extraordinary power to motivate.

I once knew a young engineer who had accumulated so much wealth that he really had no need to work again for the rest of his life. I asked him what continued to motivate him. "Keeping score," he replied. "I love beating my record."

SHARPEN YOUR GOALS

Nothing in life is more goal-oriented than sports. Ball carriers cross goal lines. Players shoot baskets. Batters get on base and score runs. Wrestlers score points for takedowns and pins. Archers hit bull's-eyes. The team or person that scores the most points wins. But in life, and in most jobs, goals are more complicated. They often aren't win or lose situations, so it's vital to know the difference between sound goals and those that are invalid.

Developing Sound Goals

The following questions will help you sharpen your present goals and set new ones that are meaningful and valid.

What's Most Important in Your Life? Robert Owen is a person you don't easily forget. He is a person with enormous charm and great wealth who currently heads seven successful businesses. His personality has won him friends worldwide and he is in demand internationally as a speaker. When I asked him the secret of his success he replied simply, "Goals." I quickly learned that he had the most unusual and complete set of personal and business goals I'd ever encountered. The areas selected for his personal and professional goals were:

Private versus business life. What ratio of time should be spent on each?

Health: What standard do I want to maintain?

Personal relationships: How can they be improved?

Education: What new fields should be pursued?

Wealth: How much should be sought?

Change of job and/or career: When and under what circumstances is a change desirable?

Social and religious life: What steps should be taken to improve quality?

Even if you don't agree with all of his priorities, you can see that Robert Owen is a man who has looked at his life and decided what is important to him.

Your own goals must be consistent with your personal values and priorities and with those of the organization for which you work. Consider, for example, the situation of the bored telephone clerk discussed earlier. She probably went right into her job at the newspaper office without talking to anyone at home or at school about her expectations in life and without even giving the matter a moment's thought. When she joined the office staff, no one thought of impressing upon her the importance of her position. She may have been the only member of that office the public would ever meet, and an explanation of the big picture could have made her feel very good about fulfilling her role with charm and efficiency. She would have begun to develop a goal for herself.

Is Everyone Involved? Whether it's your family, your team at work, or a volunteer committee in the community, everyone who will be involved in achieving a given goal should participate in setting it. This is a lesson parents often learn too late. When a camping trip gets rained out, the predictable complaints of children will be somewhat muted if they had voted on where to go and what to do on that vacation. No one wants to fail in achieving his or her goal. So the key to attaining a goal is to give some degree of responsibility for the goal to everyone who will be affected by it or involved in achieving it. To take even partial responsibility for a goal is to "own" that goal. A sense of ownership comes from partic- ipation. With ownership comes commitment. Take the mid- western trucking firm that invited me to spend a planning weekend at a remote facility far from the office phones. Each of the key managers presented his or her proposal for the best results they thought they could achieve given reasonable sup- port from the chief executive. After a weekend of reviewing, revising, and integrating each of the individual plans, the final plan was adopted. The managers said that the group effort was one of the most exhilarating experiences they had ever had. It was a first for each of them. The resulting goals were "their" goals. By participating in the process, they'd gained ownership of those goals and were committed to their accom- plishment.

What's the Best You Can Do? Goals must be demanding. A valid goal requires your best effort if it is to be motivating and rewarding. In the case of the top-producing agents who "succeeded" in spite of themselves, it became clear to them that their goals were not sufficiently demanding.

Setting demanding goals for ourselves leaves us open to the possibility of failure as well as the prospect of success. As a result, we are often tempted to set low goals to guarantee success. A salesman with a surprisingly low goal taught me the value of high goals. When I met him at the start of a seminar, his stated goal for sales in the coming year was $3 million. His previous year's sales had been $2.9 million. I asked him, only partially in jest, if $3 million was a goal or an announcement of early retirement. By the end of the seminar he decided that his goal should be $4 million. Six months after the seminar he called to say he'd raised his sights to $4.5 million on the basis of his performance since the seminar. Before the end of the year he adjusted his goal to $5 million. And he made it! And I learned a lesson I've never forgotten. Studies of peak performers have consistently shown the importance of targeting goals that demand our best.

Are Goals Do-Able? Goals must be realistic and achievable. A middle manager in a telecommunications firm asked me what I thought about bosses who assigned "outrageous" goals. I asked her what that meant. "Well," she responded, "it means he assigns tasks that are so obviously unattainable that they are ridiculous." I replied, "You've asked me what I think, and I think that it's outrageous." Goals must be realistic and attainable to prevent frustration. Nothing is more discouraging than facing tasks that are too numerous for the time available or too difficult for the abilities or resources you bring to the job.

How Can You Know When You've Achieved Goals? Goals must be measurable so that you can know when they have been accomplished. I remember a seminar attendee who set a goal of delegating more tasks to his secretary when he returned to the job. He was a state employee whom I encountered again some months later. I asked him what progress he had made in accomplishing his objective. He responded that he thought he'd done pretty well in delegating responsibility. I asked if he could be more specific. "Well, maybe they don't sound like momentous tasks," he continued, "but I've tried to give my secretary some things here and there so I wouldn't have to do them myself." "What things have you delegated?" I queried. "Well, pretty much the kind of things she can do and really ought to be doing anyway." "Like what?" I persisted. "Well," he admitted, "nothing in particular but a lot of little things in general." After a short discussion we agreed that his goal of "delegating more" was not specific and measurable. If it had been, his answers to my questions would have been far more precise. He would have said something like this: "I've delegated responsibility to my secretary for replying to all routine correspondence, for making all travel arrangements, and for screening my phone calls and visitors so that she can handle as many requests as possible herself."

Have You Set Realistic Deadlines? Goals should be deadlined. When President Kennedy announced in 1961 that America would "land a man on the moon and return him safely to the earth before this decade is out," the goal inspired the nation; it concentrated our energies and it steeled our resolution. It was a deadline set ten years into the future, and it had a profound impact not only on America but on the world. The world at that time was waiting for some signal that the United States would not surrender mastery of outer space to the Soviets.

Goals must be deadlined to be taken seriously and to provide a sense of urgency. There must be a time frame within which you will work to achieve a goal and a set time for completion. Without a deadline, a goal can hardly be taken seriously. With checkpoints or interim deadlines forcing you to monitor progress, you're much more likely to achieve your goal. If your time frame is one year and your major checkpoints are monthly, you'll have charted progress toward your goal eleven times before you reach your deadline. In many cases, monthly progress is monitored on a weekly basis and charted in a way that keeps it visible for purposes of motivation. The greatest benefits of deadlines are the sense of urgency they impart, the opportunities they present for measuring progress and taking corrective action, and the feeling of success they generate when they are met.

How Will You Keep from Forgetting? We've all lost sight of goals because they weren't written down. As mentioned earlier, we can't do what we can't remember. Yet taking time to write down goals seems to be more of an effort than many people are willing to expend. Nevertheless, the shopping list in the kitchen and the daily agenda plan on the office desk are evidence that the idea works. We wouldn't maintain them if they didn't help us. They provide a visible reminder of the things we intend to do. What we need is a system for recording goals and for scheduling checkpoints to monitor progress toward those goals at periodic intervals. Fortunately, such a system already exists and it can be applied both in the business and in the home. It will be described in Chapter 7.

What If Conditions Change? To be valid, goals must be flexible. The salesman who started with a goal of $3 million in sales and ended with $5 million adapted his goal as performance warranted. In his case, each change was an increase. When conditions change, we should be prepared to adjust our targets; but caution should be exercised in downward revisions lest we be too quick to adapt our goals when our performance slacks off. By working smarter, we may well be able to offset the downward trend instead of adapting our goals to a lower performance. This does not mean that you should wait until the outcome of your efforts is fairly obvious and then decide that this outcome was your goal. This approach is described as "shooting first and calling whatever we hit the target." It does mean, as in the case of the salesman, that you should be willing to adjust your goals up or down as changing conditions warrant. Reducing long-term goals when short-term performance lags should be done with caution and only as a last resort. If the conditions causing performance to lag are beyond your control, the case for adjusting goals downward is stronger than it would be if the cause could have been avoided. However, if new conditions make a goal unachievable, practicality dictates a review of the situation and a new determination of what is the best that can be achieved under the new conditions.

TWO GOALS—ONE PERSONAL, ONE PROFESSIONAL

Now let's consider an example of goal setting in your personal life. Say you want to participate more actively in community affairs and you have an interest in education. Accordingly, you decide to become a member of the local school board. You target as your goal becoming elected to the board of education in three years. You decide, for the sake of experience, that you will become involved in the campaign of a board member within two years. Within one year you will become familiar with the major educational issues in the school district. This week you will visit the library and a teacher friend for suggestions and resources. Note that this goal began with a long-range plan (three years) and came down to short-range specifics (this week). Let's take another example, this time a goal at work. You decide that you would like to become a department head in your company within five years. It seems logical that to do this you should become an assistant department head within two or three years. This will require getting accepted into an advancement program within one year. To prepare for that, you should take one or more supervisory development courses and score well in each of them. You will meet this week with the training director to discuss your plan and to select the courses that are best suited to your career plan. Again, note that the long-range determination must be made before it is possible to select the short-range steps that are best suited to help you achieve your long-range goal.

BALANCE YOUR WORK
AND YOUR LEISURE

Many of us successfully achieve goals at work. Increasing numbers of us do the same in regard to leisure, home, and family activities. Those who maintain a successful balance between the two are in the minority. Mike Demkiw, a very successful financial securities and insurance executive in Australia, told me of his efforts to maintain such a balance. He was taking his 10- and 11-year-old children to the hospital to bring their mother and the newly arrived baby home. The thought went through his mind that in another ten years the new baby would be the age of the children with him and these children would be gone from home. He wondered if he would know the new baby any better in the next ten years than he'd gotten to know his son and daughter in the past ten years. The fact was he hardly knew them at all. He had been almost totally preoccupied with his work. He'd been on a fast track in a fast-growth business. Wonderful opportunities had come his way, and he'd taken advantage of them. But all of this had been at a high cost: lack of time with his family.

He discussed this concern with his wife. They agreed on a change in their lifestyle. Beginning immediately, he would work normal hours instead of the very long daily hours and weekends that had characterized his work pattern up to that time. He would spend time gained with his family and would make a real effort to get to know the children better. The couple anticipated a severe impact on their income. They would sell their Mercedes, and, if necessary, they would give up their beautiful home in the suburbs.

He'd taken a time-management course, but he had applied it only partially. He knew that if he was to cushion the financial losses of such a drastic cutback in hours, he would have to do it through more effective time control. He reviewed the basics and applied them diligently. He was surprised to find himself making as much money as ever while working far fewer hours than he'd worked in the past. The family's lifestyle didn't have to change, and he got to know his children. Now he wonders why he'd waited ten years before setting a valid goal. Through improved time control he was able to balance his work and family time while achieving his goals in each area.

Bruce Peterson did a similar thing. The difference was that he set his goals in the time-management seminar itself. He targeted doubling both his sales and his family time as his goal. It took him two years. During the first year he increased his income by 50 percent and took a four-week vacation with his family instead of a two-week one, as in the past. During the second year he doubled his original income and increased his vacation time to six weeks. Bruce attributes this amazing record to setting demanding goals and to improving his time-control techniques.

Ruth A. Meyer, a manager at a *Fortune* 500 company, wrote:

> When I was a very young girl, my father said, "You don't idle well." When I was a grown woman surrounded by my family, they said, "Can't you take your pack off?" When I rode up in the elevator the other day, my former General Manager said, "We've had to hire two people to replace you—and if you'll come back, we'll combine their salaries!"
>
> At one time those comments would have made me proud. But a few years ago I began to acknowledge that my greatest challenge was to develop a balance in my life that included real relaxation, personal pursuits, the enjoyment of friendship, and spontaneity!
>
> I admit to an "unorthodox" use of your Time Tactics. It's helped the value of my time—I value myself as a personal human being outside of the work force—and has helped me develop a better balance in my life.
>
> I'm relishing daily walks—savoring the renewal of old friendships—and prioritizing by value what I want to do rather than how much I want to do! And, I started a different job in March and work regular hours!!!

These three examples brought home two important lessons to me: first, that sound time control can benefit our personal lives as much as our business lives, and, second, that the critical element in achieving both personal and business goals is time. Since this critical element is missing for most of us in our pursuit of goals, we'll deal with this missing link in the next chapter.

CHAPTER

Time—The Missing Link in Goal Pursuit

Success is doing our best. And doing our best is impossible without goals. As Chapter 2 explained, setting valid goals isn't difficult if we follow a few simple rules. But goals in themselves mean nothing until someone makes them happen. Making goals come true is hard work, which is probably why so few of them are accomplished.

Each of the successes mentioned so far contained a critical element, a link, an enabling factor that turned goals into success. That critical element was time. In most cases the factors in effective time control were learned in time-management seminars and applied with conviction to ensure that goals were accomplished. Studies indicate that the greatest reason goal setters fail to become goal getters is their inability to use time effectively. No matter how well conceived the goal, it will never be accomplished without effective use of time.

CHARGING OFF IN ALL DIRECTIONS AT ONCE

Not long ago I was having a quiet conversation with a group of people about someone who never seemed to have the time he needed to get everything done. With a seemingly offhand remark, one participant cited a recent incident: "As usual, he went charging off in all directions at once." Of course, we've all made that comment at some time about someone. In fact, the expression is so common that no one even asks what it means. Yet going in more than one direction at a time is obviously impossible. The gap between the behavior described and reality attests to the bizarre impression such behavior creates. What lies behind it? Can we pinpoint its causes? And what does it tell us about time?

Overenthusiasm or fear and anxiety will often result in hasty, ill-conceived action. How often does an idea pop into your mind prompting you to do something in haste that later proves not to be in your own or others' best interests? Most of us are prone to this kind of behavior when we're under stress.

In crisis situations how often do we overreact, thinking that speed is critical? Cooler heads would ask: "What is the worst that can happen if no action is taken immediately?" Those who charge off in all directions confuse motion with accomplishment, activity with results. They would do better if they clarified their priorities and targeted their achievement, beginning with their most important priorities first.

Running Out of Time

People who seem to be charging off in all directions at once usually share a common characteristic: They complain about not having enough time. Their remedy for the problem is to run faster rather than to work smarter. They fail to recognize the fundamental paradox of time: No one has enough, yet everyone has all there is.

TENTACLES OF TIME

Time pervades all that we do or think. Its silent tentacles continuously intrude upon our lives. Nothing we do at work or at leisure escapes its clutch. After all, we can do nothing that doesn't take time. In my work on time management I have come to realize that there are three important factors in life that omit considerations of time: productivity, workaholism, and stress.

Productivity and Time

Productivity, in the language of the engineer, is the ratio of output to input. For example, if a well-tuned engine has enough fuel for 100 miles of driving but uses it all in only 30 miles, the productivity (efficiency) of that engine would be its output divided by its input, that is, 30/100, or 30 percent.

The cost-benefit ratio is a common approach used in analyzing large projects; the benefit is the output, and the cost is the input. Thus, productivity = output/input = benefit/cost.

Time can be viewed as one of the costs (or inputs) of every task, and the results can be viewed as the benefit (or output). Hence, the productivity of a task = results/time. Suppose we want to improve the productivity of our meetings, one of the most prevalent of time wasters. If we could cut our meeting time in half and achieve comparable results, we would be doubling our productivity in meetings as follows:

Productivity = results/time = 100/.5 = 200

Accordingly, in any area of human activity, if we want to double our productivity, we can do so by achieving comparable results in half the time. The implications of this finding are rather startling when we realize that the quest for improved productivity has neglected the factor of personal productivity of individuals. Although the connection between personal time and productivity is irrefutable, it has apparently not yet been taken seriously by organizations in either the private or the public sector.

Workaholism and Time

Time and workaholism seem linked in a rather perverse way. *Workaholics*, as defined by Dr. Marilyn Machlowitz, are those "whose desire to work long and hard is intrinsic and whose work habits almost always exceed the prescriptions of the job they do and the expectations of the people with whom or for whom they work."* Machlowitz's study drew some surprising conclusions: (1) Workaholics tend to be healthier, to be happier, and to live longer than others. (2) Workaholics are unlikely to change, so the problem is whether those living with them are able to adapt.

What this seems to suggest is that workaholics themselves don't suffer as much as those around them. Their seemingly bizarre time-management practices inflict pain on others, not themselves. I've always loved my work of writing and speaking on subjects of keen interest to me, and I've often thought how difficult it must be to hate one's work. But now I see that my workaholic tendencies did inflict pain on family members, for example, when work took precedence over family activities. In retrospect, I would like to have known much more about

---

* Dr. Marilyn Machlowitz, *Workaholics: Living with Them, Working with Them*, Addison-Wesley, Reading, Mass., 1980.

workaholism and to have been able to correct my tendencies. I wish I'd known that "liking my work" was irrelevant to the question of whether I was a workaholic. I wish I'd known that workaholism represents compulsive behavior similar to drug dependency, overeating, and gambling and that steps can be taken to modify that behavior and the attitudes supporting it.

It is most important to realize that the goal of achieving a balance between work life and home life may, in the case of the workaholic, be sacrificed unnecessarily on the altar of compulsive behavior. The problem faced by potential workaholics and their families is that, for many, there is no question of what comes first when a conflict occurs between work and personal life. In fact, there is essentially no conflict. Work comes first, whether it be work engaged in at a paid job or work pursued for its own sake to the detriment of family relationships and recreational activities.

There is hope, however, for persons who want to avoid the workaholic trap. They must seriously target the goal of a balanced life—work and home, family, leisure. Individuals who determine what is important to them and make time-management decisions accordingly are usually those who experience the fewest time-control pressures and problems.

Stress and Time

Time and stress—an unlikely duo? No. Not when we realize that most of our concerns with time represent *stressors*. In the next three chapters we will be examining three categories of time wasters. Everything that wastes our time places us under the additional stress of not having enough time, so every potential time waster is also a potential stressor.

The value of seeing this connection clearly was brought home to me by a recent article on stress. The article posed the case of a manager whose discussion with a visitor is interrupted by a phone call. The article proposes that the manager needs to know techniques for coping with the stress generated by this interruption. A better approach than coping *after* it happens is to prevent it before it happens. Sound time management permits this through the technique of "screening" calls. A well-trained secretary could answer the phone call and determine whether it is important enough to warrant interrupting the manager.

One of the approaches above is remedial; the other is preventive. Understanding the linkage between time and stress can pay dividends by alerting us to the possibility of preventing stress rather than searching for a cure after it has occurred.

It's becoming clear that stress has a great deal to do with our control—or lack of control—of time. For many of us, indeed, time is our master. We seem to have little power over it.

> Alice sighed wearily, "I think you might do something better with the time," she said, "than waste it in asking riddles that have no answers." "If you know time as well as I do," said the Hatter, "you wouldn't talk about wasting it. It's him." "I don't know what you mean," said Alice. "Of course you don't!" said the Hatter, tossing his head contemptuously. "I dare say you never ever spoke to Time!" said the Hatter. "Perhaps not," Alice cautiously replied, "but I know I have to beat time when I learn music." "Ah! That accounts for it," said the Hatter. "He won't stand beating. Now, if you only kept on good terms with him, he'd do almost anything you like (with the clock)."*

We all know what it feels like to run out of time. We panic, we grow anxious, and often we become bad-tempered and hard to live or work with. The stress it occasions is manifested in everyday situations. We see it in the student who has a long, tough homework assignment that still needs pages of

---

* Lewis Carroll, *Alice's Adventures in Wonderland.*

work as the clock ticks past bedtime. We see it in the home-maker who has piles of clothes that still need to be washed as the weekend away from home rapidly approaches. We see it in the office manager who has last-minute extra typing that needs to be done as his superior anxiously awaits an update on sales.

"TIME WASTERS"

Since the above-mentioned people started the week, or the day, with exactly the same amount of time as the next person, we can conclude that at some point they "wasted" their time, or spent it unwisely for no reward. We might even describe them as "time wasters." But let's look more closely at the examples. The student, the homemaker, and the office manager are all conscientious, hardworking people. How can we properly call them time wasters? Let's shift our perspective and consider instead the obstacles that prevent these individuals from working most effectively, that is, from getting maximum results in minimum time. Let's agree to call these obstacles the "time wasters," rather than applying the label haphazardly to human beings. While it is clear that some people are much more effective than others, it is equally clear that we all waste *some* time periodically. When such an occasion arises, it is usually obstacles, or time wasters, that are preventing us from achieving our objectives most effectively. We tend to run out of time. Since this puts us under stress, we conclude that any time waster, according to our new definition, will be a direct cause of this stress.

Manage Time for Success

The effective use of time is critical to the accomplishment of goals. And goal achievement is essential for success. So individuals who want to be successful must be effective time managers. Unfortunately, there are a lot of impediments to the effective control of time wasters. The good news is that once time wasters are identified, their causes are fairly obvious and solutions are not difficult to implement.

My study of time use has taken me to forty countries on five continents. Table 1, on pages 44–45, lists the top twenty time wasters worldwide and shows their relative ranking in various geographic regions. Note that the top six time concerns never rank below seventh in any part of the world. This is particularly impressive as these rankings are a composite of a large number of individual rankings chosen from a list of forty time concerns.

CATEGORIES OF TIME CONCERNS

For sharper distinction and easier analysis, the top twenty time concerns can be divided into three broad categories, as shown below. World rankings from the table are given in parentheses after each time concern. Two concerns appear without rankings, as they were not among the table's top twenty. The classification highlights the broad applicability of the concerns, encompassing business as well as personal activities. The first category, "Human Time Barriers," sounds so close to home that we may feel we should have most control over these concerns. Yet they may well be the most challenging time concerns to overcome, since they involve that notoriously intractable concept, human nature. The second category, "Managerial Time Barriers," is concerned with managerial skills that, when neglected, cause significant waste of time for everyone. These skills are easy for people who have mastered them, more difficult for those who have not. The third category, "Environmental Time Barriers," consists of time concerns that are easy to spot and relatively simple to remedy. Let's review the time wasters in each category; then we will examine them in greater detail in succeeding chapters.

Human Time Barriers

- ♦ Attempting too much (6)
- ♦ Personal disorganization; cluttered desk (8)
- ♦ Inability to say "no" (9)
- ♦ Lack of self-discipline (10)
- ♦ Procrastination; indecision (11)
- ♦ Leaving tasks unfinished (15)
- ♦ Socializing (19)

Managerial Time Barriers

- ♦ Crisis management; shifting priorities (2)
- ♦ Lack of objectives, priorities, planning (3)
- ♦ Ineffective delegation (5)
- ♦ Untrained or inadequate staff (12)
- ♦ Lack of, or unclear, communication (16)
- ♦ Confused responsibility or authority (18)
- ♦ Lack of standards, controls, progress reports (20)
- ♦ Not listening

Environmental Time Barriers

- ♦ Telephone interruptions (1)

Table 1. Professionals' Top 20 Time Concerns Worldwide

	U.S.A.	Canada	Latin America	Europe	Asia	Australia
1. Telephone interruptions	2	1	1	1	2	3
2. Crisis management; shifting priorities	1	2	7	4	6	2
3. Lack of objectives, priorities, planning	3	4	3	6	5	1
4. Drop-in visitors	5	5	2	5	4	6
5. Ineffective delegation	6	6	4	2	1	7
6. Attempting too much	4	3	6	3	7	4
7. Meetings	11	8	5	7	3	12
8. Personal disorganization; cluttered desk	7	7	9	8	10	5
9. Inability to say "no"	9	9	11	9	9	9

10. Lack of self-discipline	10	19	11	17	10	8
11. Procrastination; indecision	8	17	13	16	11	10
12. Untrained or inadequate staff	14	12	10	10	16	13
13. Incomplete or delayed information	20	8	14	8	—	20
14. Paperwork; red tape; reading	13	—	17	15	12	12
15. Leaving tasks unfinished	11	13	12	—	14	13
16. Lack of, or unclear, communication	—	11	16	12	19	18
17. Understaffed; overstaffed	—	20	19	14	14	16
18. Confused responsibility or authority	16	13	15	18	17	17
19. Socializing	15	—	—	—	15	15
20. Lack of standards, controls, progress reports	18	18	—	13	—	—

♦ Drop-in visitors (4)

♦ Meetings (7)

♦ Incomplete or delayed information (13)

♦ Paperwork; red tape; reading (14)

♦ Understaffed; overstaffed (17)

♦ Noise; visual distractions

HUMAN TIME BARRIERS

I chanced upon the human category of time concerns in talking with a hospital administrator in New Jersey. Having given considerable thought to the problems of time management, he concluded, "Time management has the virtue of simplicity, but it is terribly difficult to carry out because it goes against human nature." It was clear that certain time concerns such as procrastination, personal disorganization, lack of self-discipline, and the desire to socialize are related to human nature or human characteristics. They are natural tendencies likely to be found to some extent in everyone.

Later I had the opportunity of conducting a series of seminars for the Canadian Bar Association. As a lawyer myself, I reflected before the meeting on the possibility that these lawyers might be reluctant to identify their personal time wasters. They might feel that to do so would be self-deprecating, since their time, along with their skills and knowledge, of course, was the basis of their billings to their clients. Facing 100 lawyers at the first session, I gave them a team assignment: The members of each team were to list as many human characteristics of lawyers as they could think of that adversely affected lawyers' management of time. Contrary to my expectations, lively discussions ensued at every table. More than thirty characteristics were identified. Among the more interesting were indecision (from being trained to see both sides of issues), loquaciousness, file hoarding (from the desire to maintain control over client accounts), and accepting unrealistic requests from clients (from an excessive desire to please).

Time wasters based on human characteristics are thought to be the most difficult kind of time barrier to master because they deal with our inherent nature and the habits of a lifetime. On the other hand, we have more opportunity to work on these time concerns because we can make choices about our own conduct on a more or less continuing basis once we have identified them. Surely, we ought to be able to exercise more control over our own behavior than that of others or our environment.

In the worldwide time-waster profile in Table 1, human time barriers rank lower, in general, than do neglected managerial skills and environmental factors. This may reflect a reluctance to look at ourselves first as a likely cause of our own problems. It's easier to see time wasting in the behavior of others and to feel that our problems are primarily caused by others or by our environment. In seminars, the initial perception of time concerns among the participants appears to give a much heavier weight to environmental factors than to human characteristics. When we review this original perception later in the seminar, we usually discover a strong trend toward ranking personal or human time barriers much higher. For example, the participants at one seminar initially failed to rank "lack of self-discipline" among their top ten time concerns. At the end of the second day, its overall ranking rose to first place. As noted above, we tend at first to ignore our own shortcomings. When considered among other time concerns, however, lack of self-discipline becomes a significant concern.

Personal disorganization is often a basis for humor. Take the things we misplace. Surely, most of us lose something, even if only temporarily, almost everyday. So common is this problem that it has spawned a body of jokes and cartoons. One wit observed how strange it is that the hardest to find are the things we put where they can't get lost. Another universal problem is leaving things where we last used them instead of putting them back where they belong. One popular sign reads: "Don't put it down. Put it back!" Few of us have photographic memories as to where we laid something in a hurry. Losing papers—whether they are on a cluttered desk, in a disorganized file, or in the wrong place—costs time and often causes great inconvenience and even harm to the persons depending on the timely delivery of those papers.

Another human time barrier, attempting too much, has many ramifications. It leads to missing deadlines, working under pressure, making errors in judgment, and wasting the time of those who depend on us for timely cooperation.

When we say "yes" too often to others' requests, we frequently find ourselves doing their work and neglecting our own. Except for requests with a higher priority, saying "yes" makes little sense when we ourselves have too much to do in too little time.

The tendency to leave tasks unfinished when we are interrupted causes problems later when we pick those tasks up again and try to figure out in what state we left them. My studies show that in many cases it takes three times as long to recover from an interruption as it does to endure it. It is likely that the loss of time involved in recovering from interruptions and completing unfinished tasks far exceeds our assumptions.

The vital difference between time using and time wasting is exemplified by socializing. Like humor, socializing can serve a business purpose by putting people at ease, enlisting someone's help in getting to his or her boss, or perhaps easing the tension in a given situation. Taken too far, however, it is a great time waster. Socializing is also a primary element in three other major time concerns (telephone interruptions, drop-in visitors, and meetings), each of which ranks much higher (first, fourth, and seventh, respectively) on the world-wide list.

Finally, we come to procrastination. Is it coincidental that this human time concern is discussed last? Putting things off is such a universal behavior that it's been dubbed "the human condition." And rightly so. Ask yourself how many things at home—and at work—you had planned to have finished by this time but have put off for one reason or another.

My favorite rationale for putting things off has always been that I work best under pressure. Or so I thought. My wife, however, never welcomed the pressure of impending dead-lines. She habitually reminds me of deadlines well in advance and asks why I don't get started on projects early to avoid last-minute pressure. Initially, I resisted, saying that since I worked best under pressure there should be no problem. Beginning a project early seemed an intrusion on my freedom to enjoy myself, especially if the project's deadline was a long way off. One day we talked about procrastination on the way to the airport. Preparations for the trip had been another crisis situation filled with last-minute discoveries and changes that could easily have been anticipated if I'd started planning ear-lier rather than leaving everything till the last day. Something my wife said at that time has stuck with me. "Maybe you can stand the pressure," she said, "but for those you leave behind, it's a different story. Your staff are really glad to see you go because things can get back to normal. If you could see the looks on their faces when you race out the door, you'd change your mind about the effect this last-minute-itis has on others."

I still have difficulty starting any project as far in advance as I should. But I now see the benefits more clearly: more time to think a problem through, to get opinions of others, to look up facts, to correct a mistake if one is discovered. And this means higher-quality results in the end.

Human time barriers are deeply ingrained, but they can be overcome. Chapter 4 explains how to do this.

MANAGERIAL TIME BARRIERS

Managerial time barriers are those that occur because of neglected managerial skills. Proper employment of these skills is not confined to an office. In our personal activities we can often identify a situation in which the lack of proper management has brought about near disaster. Consider, perhaps, the vacation you failed to plan in advance. You arrived at the only ferry to Block Island. The names of people in the cars ahead had been checked off on a list by a guard who tells you that your name is not on his list. He asks you if you have a reservation on the ferry. "What reservation?" you ask, hoping he is kidding. "The one you need to get on this ferry," he responds dryly. "Well, I didn't know you needed one," you reply weakly. "Sure do," he says. "Please pull out of the line and check with the lady in the office to see if there are any openings left for next week." "But," you protest, "we have a house reserved on the island for *this* week." You hope the touch of agony in your voice will be unmistakable. "Sorry," he says; "please pull over now so we can load the rest of the cars." This unfortunate incident actually happened to me and my family, but all of us can describe situations in which the lack of advance planning led to embarrassment, humiliation, and even shock. What was *your* worst lack-of-planning experience?

Planning ahead is hard work, and it takes time. Since most of us feel we don't have enough time as it is, we don't like to spend it planning. For most of us long-range planning is akin to asking, "Where are we going for lunch?" Winston Churchill commented wisely on our tendency toward short-sighted planning when he said, "It is difficult to look into the future further than you can see."

Remember the hostages in Iran and the rescue debacle? Did somebody forget to ask what could go wrong? Wouldn't it occur to someone experienced in desert flying that sandstorms might disable some of the helicopters? There was an instance of short-sighted planning on an international scale. My Block Island fiasco was an instance of short-sighted domestic planning. If I had asked what could go wrong on the trip, the ferry reservation would certainly have come to mind and the vacation would have been much better.

Contingency planning goes beyond basic planning. It involves identifying the potential pitfalls of a plan and then taking steps to prevent the most serious and likely of those contingencies from occurring or to limit the consequences if they do occur. Planning a trip to Block Island, for example, should include—among other things—making a ferry reservation; contingency planning would include realizing that the ferry company might lose that reservation and taking steps to minimize the likelihood that this will happen. You would save the receipt for your deposit, and perhaps you would phone a week ahead to confirm the reservation. The call might cost you a couple of dollars, but a rented vacation house you couldn't use will cost hundreds.

We're told the plan for Iran first called for thirty-six helicopters. But the thinkers in the White House war room were concerned that such a large number of helicopters might be easily detected, so the number was cut to eighteen and then to nine. No one asked, it seems, if there were conditions in the desert that could knock out helicopter engines. As it happened, sandstorms ruined several engines. Of the operational helicopters, two collided. The mission failed, and the United States took a beating in the press. The mission took months to plan. A British specialist in hostage rescue said the United States should have taken the Israelis up on their offer to loan the Americans the finest trained and most experienced rescue team in the world.

Yes, plan for contingencies. Always ask what can go wrong.

What else? What else? Then ask how these potential problems can be avoided. If they can't be avoided, ask how the consequences can be limited.

Among neglected managerial skills is delegation. Let's tune in to the musings of one who has observed a manager who doesn't delegate. "The do-it-yourselfer did himself in again. He doesn't trust anyone. Has to get it right. Starts to give it to you, then takes it back. Says 'Well, on second thought, I guess I'd better do this myself. You know, the boss has to have it just so.' So now he's doing everything himself. Kind of nice for us, but dumb for him. He's working ten, twelve hours a day and half the weekend and wondering why we're always going home on time. Getting himself in trouble too. Yesterday he missed a big deadline. Top customer order didn't get out. Huge crisis, and he couldn't find anyone to blame. He'd done it all himself. We could have prevented it, if he'd only let us do what we're paid to do. Well, that's the way he wants it. Someday he'll learn to delegate." Is delegation easy? No. Do-able? Yes. Can it be learned? Of course. Is it neglected? All the time. Is it vital? Absolutely, if you want to manage.

There will be more on these and other neglected managerial skills that cost time when we get to Chapter 5.

ENVIRONMENTAL TIME BARRIERS

In this category are the highest-ranked time concerns in the world. Paradoxically, they are the easiest to solve, as the examples below indicate.

The Telephone

The telephone rings. The world's number-one time waster is about to strike again. In the film *Managing Time** the man-

---

*Peter Drucker, *Managing Time*, Bureau of National Affairs.

ager reaches for the phone, but his secretary, who is making a few notes at his desk, picks it up first. He looks a little nervous about not handling his own phone. He likes answering his own phone. It makes him feel important, and it's nice to help people out. He doesn't realize he's taking calls others are being paid to answer. He doesn't realize the calls are keeping him from achieving his own goals for the day. He has no idea how much time this wastes. His people know. They keep waiting for the papers he hasn't reviewed, the decisions he hasn't made. And he wonders where his day has gone— at 10 p.m. he has to turn out the lights and lock the doors. This is his place. He owns it. And the business too. He doesn't realize he's killing his team's initiative and sense of self-worth. Sure, he has a few reasons for not delegating the screening of calls, but deep down he knows they don't quite hold water. He's glad no one has pressed him on it. They could tell him, if he'd let them. Worst of all, he doesn't realize he's a doer, not a manager.

The telephone is part of everyone's environment these days. Its ring can invade our thoughts at work, or our domestic privacy, with an urgency unequaled by any other interruption. Here is an environmental time barrier that makes itself extremely obvious. Fortunately, it is one we can readily overcome by observing a few easy rules.

On the domestic scene, long-winded callers who ring at unexpected hours while the homemaker is busy with chores pose a very different problem. We've encountered several innovative devices that offer a solution. One is an extra-long cord installed on the kitchen phone, which enables the listener to walk about as necessary while continuing the conversation. Another is a bell installed near the phone that sounds as if someone is at the door, which makes it easy to break off with: "Can I call you back?"

Drop-In Visitors

"Have you got a minute" queries the voice at your office door. Without looking up, you say, "Sure, come in." You ask no questions such as "What's it about," or "Could so-and-so help you with that," or "Would tomorrow be okay?" You just say, "Come in." Drop-in visitors have been interrupting you all your life, and you've done little to restrict their entry on even a limited basis. You've made little effort to sort out their relative priorities or to discover whether they've tried to solve their problems themselves or to get help elsewhere. Drop-in visitors, the world's number-four time waster, have a fascination all their own. The extent to which drop-in visitors—at work, at home, and at leisure—infringe upon our use of time is far greater than most of us imagine. The "open-door" policy has, ironically, aggravated this problem. It has taken us a long time to see the wisdom of closing our doors.

Meetings

"What do you mean, the meeting's over? I just found myself a comfortable chair." Meetings. Meetings. Meetings. With all that's been written about them, all the jokes that ridicule them, all the pleas to shorten or eliminate them, they still persist. Meetings rank seventh among time wasters worldwide. Imagine where they would rank if each person realized it isn't just his or her own time being wasted at a meeting but also the time of everyone else in attendance. In addition, the attendees' salaries must be factored in, as well as the opportunity cost that results when workers are unavailable to others because they are at meetings. Dr. Kenneth Dunn, one of the great former superintendents in the state of New York, was a creative time manager who had little patience with meetings that wasted time. He put a big clock face with a single minute hand on the wall of his conference room; the face was marked so that the hand would read the "minutes remaining" in the meeting. "Everyone could see it. It had a direct impact on meetings. Everyone became conscious that the clock was watching, relentlessly ticking off the minutes remaining." Dr. Dunn didn't just understand the problem—he did something about it.

These and other environmental time barriers will be discussed in detail in Chapter 6, where I'll present proven techniques for conquering each of them. For now, let's turn to an in-depth look at the human characteristics that are so critical in goal achievement and hence in success.

C H A P T E R

Breaking Human Time Barriers

Because human time barriers are so much a part of us, we are slow to recognize them for what they really are: the principal obstacles to our control of time. Overcoming these obstacles is a multistep process. First, we must acknowledge that these barriers originate in our own shortcomings. If we are honest enough to admit this, we can begin to overcome them. Willpower alone won't be enough—although without it nothing else will be of any use. We need to change the way we do certain things, and we need practical help to do so. Second, we must choose a systematic approach to revising our behavior and, having chosen it, must use it to help us find solutions.

Now let's look at the human time barriers in the order in which they have been ranked worldwide:

1. Attempting too much (6)

2. Personal disorganization; cluttered desk (8)

3. Inability to say "no" (9)

4. Lack of self-discipline (10)

5. Procrastination; indecision (11)

6. Leaving tasks unfinished (15)

7. Socializing (19)

ATTEMPTING TOO MUCH

Do you ever feel that you've been taking on too much? Have you been too quick to say "yes" to requests of others? You are not alone. Trying to do it all is very common. It ranks number six as a barrier to success. (This tendency is very common in the business world, but we can expect it to occur with at least the same frequency in our domestic lives, in our social lives, and in the lives of our children. After all, this is a human characteristic, so there is no reason to suspect otherwise.) Even if we don't attempt too much ourselves, we have certainly all met someone who does.

Whenever an activity is planned or a job needs doing, for example, you can expect someone to say, "Let's ask Mary if she'll do it." Mary is a single parent and an officer in several volunteer organizations. In addition, she has a full-time job. She is fairly well organized, but she takes on too many tasks. The volunteer organizations seem to languish under her leadership even though she attends all the meetings and agrees that "we ought to do something about this." Projects have a way of getting grounded due to inattention when she is the project leader. She is good at her job and makes a good wage, but her promotion keeps getting postponed. Her boss believes that Mary lacks that extra something it takes to be a leader. And Mary's home life verges on chaotic. The kids do their share, but the house is always short on groceries and long on messiness. Saturdays are spent trying to catch up. By Sunday night the family is tired and irritable. Teachers meet frequently with Mary to discuss why the children are not performing up to their obvious potential.

Let's be clear. It isn't that Mary doesn't know how to say "no." She refused to canvass for the heart fund "because she didn't have time." And she said there would be no Disneyland during spring break because she had too much to do at work to take a vacation. Mary's trouble is that she thinks she *can* do it all. Because she could always see what needed to be done, to her the job was as good as completed. With a young son and daughter, she was a natural as the member of the book committee who would recommend children's books to the library. Unfortunately, she never found the time to draw up the list. Mary lacks goals, as we defined them in Chapter 1. She is overambitious and overconfident, and she fails to schedule her time realistically. Perhaps she is insecure and feels that her importance comes from being involved in many things instead of doing a few really well. Mary is a trooper when someone has an emergency, even when it means dropping something that might be more important. But instead of feeling good about her accomplishments, Mary lacks a sense of achievement. She tends to confuse motion with progress and activity with results. She wears herself out and then wonders what she achieved.

With a system such as Time Tactics* Mary might have a chance. Her daily plan would show her the top priorities for the day, and time would be set aside for their accomplishment. Her whole week would be scheduled, and she could see it all at one glance. This could give her a ready reason to say "no" to less important opportunities and requests that didn't fit her priorities. Her advance monthly calendars would provide a place for noting future commitments so that they would not

---

*See Appendix, p. 171.

come as a big surprise. By focusing on the priority of meeting her goals, she'll always get the most important things done. She'll waste far less effort and conserve her energy for things that really matter. Her projects could be time-lined on project sheets to facilitate monitoring progress at periodic intervals. Contact logs would permit her to make notes while talking to a potential committee member; later, she could instantly determine exactly where the conversation ended if she needed this information. She'd feel better about delegating and do it more often because she would have a convenient way of tracking the tasks she gives to others. She'll be attempting less but getting more done through systematic accomplishment of her goals, both personal and business.

PERSONAL DISORGANIZATION;
CLUTTERED DESK

During a conversation I had in Heidelberg on the subject of the "cluttered desk" phenomenon, a German manager leaned forward intently and asked: "Herr doctor, do you know *why* we stack our desks with so much paperwork?" I replied that from his tone of voice I suspected that I didn't. "Why *do* we stack our desks?" I asked. "Well," he continued, "it's all those things that are so important we don't want to forget them. So we leave them on top of our desks where we'll see them. The trouble is it works too well. Every time our gaze wanders from what we're working on to those things we didn't want to forget, we remember them, and we forget what we're working on!"

Chronically disorganized people are liabilities to themselves and to others who depend on them for timely, reliable information and decisions. The term "liability" may not be strong enough. Anyone who is disorganized—whether a salesperson or a president, a parent or a child—has a disruptive effect on others. Deadlines are missed; promised actions are delayed; time is wasted searching for lost notes and misplaced files. For a number of reasons the problem doesn't lend itself to easy solutions. Yet managers who *are* organized make becoming so seem easy. Albert Grenier, the youngest participant in a seminar for chief executives in Europe, headed one of the fastest-growing and most successful companies in Germany at that time, yet he worked only thirty-five hours per week! When I asked him how he managed that, he looked puzzled. After musing a moment, he replied:

> It's just managing well; knowing where you are going with clearly defined objectives and a good plan to achieve them; selecting competent people and motivating them through proper delegation and communication; and measuring progress at pre-determined checkpoints to ensure that performance conforms to plans. When you do this well, there is no need for long hours. You can lead a well-rounded life and you should. It's the only way to ensure success in the long run.

Albert Grenier was speaking for those managers who know the fundamentals and stick to them. They don't believe that managers have to work long hours to succeed. They feel that by working long hours they are admitting that they cannot get their jobs done during the normal working day or that they don't know how to say "no" to unreasonable task demands. They would agree with Engstrom and Juroe, authors of *The Work Trap*, who call workaholism the only addiction that has been permitted to masquerade as a virtue instead of a vice.

Why does getting and staying organized seem so simple for some and so difficult for others?

The first step in staying organized is to understand why many of us resist getting organized in the first place. Some feel that organization represents a loss of freedom; for them, a cleared desk and a place for everything mean rigid conformity that threatens spontaneity and creativity. Objectives and deadlines are looked upon as mandating accountability and ending freedom to do the things one wants to do. Many individuals fail to recognize that good organization frees a person to do the things he or she would otherwise not have time for.

It's clear that a fulfilling personal life is an accomplished goal for some and an elusive concept for others. Explaining the cause of personal frustrations, disorganized people often say, "I guess I just don't live right." The good news is that there is a better way to live. The use of an integrated system for personal organization will allow us to exact a great degree of control over the management of our own time. Such a system is an invaluable tool. However, it is one thing to manage ourselves and our own time requirements, but it is quite another to develop skills in relation to other people's demands on our time. In this area we encounter another human time waster, the inability to say "no."

INABILITY TO SAY "NO"

At some time, every one of us has said "yes" and then wished we had said "no." Perhaps the greatest single cause of not saying "no" when we should is a lack of clear priorities. Of course, we want to help others and to win approval. Afraid of offending others, we say "yes" to every request and find ourselves lost in a deluge of commitments we cannot meet. People are disappointed and angry; we become depressed and frustrated. Even when we recognize the problem, getting the little word "no" out of our mouths seems impossible.

Here are four steps that will enable you to say "no" whenever it is appropriate:

1. *Listen* to the request attentively. Let the speaker explain what is needed without interruption. In this way,

he or she knows that you are fully informed and able to give the matter your serious consideration. If the person making the request is not given a chance to explain its importance, you may say "no" prematurely or even erroneously—you may miss a good reason for saying "yes."

2. Say *"no"* if the request is one you should decline. Don't hesitate with "maybe" or "I'm really very busy." A simple "No, I'm sorry, I won't be able to do that" should suffice in the great majority of cases. Many people making such requests expect a "no"; they are genuinely surprised when they get a "yes."

3. Give the *reasons* for your answer if you feel an explanation will help. "I've got a deadline that will take the rest of the day to meet," or "I'm not the right person for this task," or perhaps "Other commitments won't permit my helping with that, though I wish I could."

4. Offer *alternatives*, if possible, to demonstrate good faith. Try "Have you thought about asking Charlie?" or "If it can wait until tomorrow, I can give you an hour of my time then."

Listen, no, reasons, alternatives. List these key terms on a card and tape it to your telephone; you'll see them every time you start to say "yes" when you should be saying "no."

Keep in mind what happened the last time you said "yes" when you should have said "no." A friend of mine well remembers the time her daughter came home and said: "Mom, can you drive the luggage to the 4-H camp? There are too many kids on the bus and they don't have room." Wanting to show her support for the camp, which was very inexpensive, my friend said, "Of course." The camp, it turned out, was six hours away, which meant twelve hours of driving in one day.

What her daughter hadn't taken into account was that this job was often done by a couple who enjoyed spending the night at the camp before they returned home. They were miffed over being displaced. So who was happy and grateful? My friend is not likely to forget that you never say "yes" until you're absolutely certain that "no" is the wrong answer.

LACK OF SELF-DISCIPLINE

By now it is obvious that human time barriers can be overcome. We can learn to limit our commitments. We can learn to clear our desktops of accumulated clutter and to integrate our plans, memos, and records in an organized system. We can learn to say "no" to requests we know we cannot or should not fulfill. These techniques, however, all demand self-discipline.

Many people express surprise that lack of self-discipline is identified as one of the human barriers to success. "Isn't that the whole story?" they ask. Well, insofar as good management depends on good habits, and self-discipline is a powerful habit affecting many of the other time barriers, the answer is a partial "yes." Self-discipline is fundamental to sound management and therefore to sound time management.

We sometimes hear people say: "I'm the creative type. Self-discipline is not my bag. No wonder I'm disorganized." This is a rationalization that sounds suspiciously like self-satisfaction. And it's misplaced. Creativity is not confusion, nor is it fostered by confusion. In fact, creativity involves bringing order out of chaos. Self-discipline is one of the greatest assets of the creative person. Dr. Eleanor Schwartz, vice-chancellor of academic affairs at the University of Missouri School of Business, is one of the most creative and prolific writers I have known. She is also one of the most disciplined, with a regimen of early morning writing that starts long before most of us would even think of getting up. Many successful writers have testified to the powerful effect of disciplining themselves to start writing at the same time each day.

If you are not naturally self-disciplined, you can form habits that will make up for your lack of self-discipline. And forming the habit of acting as if you were disciplined is the quickest way to eradicate this powerful barrier to success. Take your goals seriously and write them down; write a plan for every day and follow it. Recognize the universal tendency to put the easy and pleasant task ahead of the unpleasant but necessary task. We joke that the roof doesn't need fixing when it isn't raining and can't be fixed when it is raining. But if we eventually fix the roof, it'll be on a nice day; and postponing the job will probably result in having to redo the ceiling underneath!

Recognize that lack of planning encourages undisciplined action and, conversely, that sound planning encourages disciplined action. Plan your work; then work your plan. Impose realistic but firm deadlines on yourself and expect them of others. If you tend to disregard your own deadlines, announce them publicly and enlist the aid of others in keeping them.

The greatest aid to self-discipline is a good organizational tool such as Time Tactics. Set interim deadlines and check your progress periodically against your final deadlines. Chart your progress and keep your chart visible as a constant reminder of how you are doing and what actions are required to keep on target. Learn to say "no" to requests that divert your energy from your own priorities and to requests for which the requestor has alternative courses of action. Practice completing tasks and handling things at your desk only once.

PROCRASTINATION; INDECISION

Have you ever wondered why it's actually fun to put things off or, at least, why doing so gives you a pleasant feeling? It must be that we like choices. I can do this, if I like, or I can do that. Choices make us feel powerful, as if we have control over our destiny. We can decide *not* to do something we know needs doing, or we can at least decide not to do it right now. Yes, we like having the freedom to choose. What we don't like is our inability to avoid the consequences of our choices.

For me, procrastination started when I was in college. The semester grade for each subject was determined primarily by a student's final-exam score. I would put off reviewing for the finals for as long as possible. Then, shortly before the exams, I would assess the situation: Many exams coming up; extensive review necessary for most of them; not enough time; stay up late; drink coffee and take No Doz tablets to stay awake. When the day of an exam finally came, I was too tired to do well. Afterward, I would compare my results with others. The top scorers were usually the students who did their studying and reviewing as they went along. They didn't wait till the end, when there wasn't enough time. If they didn't understand something, they would look into it at the time and ask questions of other students or the teacher until they understood it.

Every time we choose one course of action, we automatically exclude another. We'll never know for sure, but the excluded action might have yielded more attractive results than the course we followed. So when we make a choice, we should figure in the *opportunity cost*—that is, the potential value of the opportunities lost because of our choice. If we choose to let things slide, for the pleasure of the moment, at least we should make our decision consciously.

We put things off for a host of reasons: uncertainty over how others will respond, lack of confidence in the outcome, and even simple laziness. A homemaker chooses not to clean out the closet but to finish a gripping detective story. A homeowner chooses not to call the town supervisor right away but to fix the car. Another homeowner chooses not to speak to the neighbors about their noisy dog but to sit in the den which faces away from their yard. A reporter chooses not to ask the boss for a pay raise but to update the file of contacts' names and phone numbers.

When we examine these choices, we see four people who are not in command of their lives. Take the homemaker. He knows the closet is bulging with coats, brooms, schoolbags, egg cartons, and dirty rags. Yet he closes the door and busies himself with a book. In command? No. Lazy? Yes. And unwilling to face the consequences of starting the task. After all, once the stuff is out of the closet, there's thorough cleaning to be done, decisions to be made about what to throw out, and places to be found for a diversity of articles. One thing will lead to another, and maybe other closets will need reorganization too. Who needs *that*?

Then there's the homeowner faced with an unwelcome development in town. It may mean the loss of the open field and wetlands where she and her friends have always enjoyed their leisure. But she's not very good at explaining things, nor is she the one to stick her neck out and speak for other people. She may sound like a fool or give offense. That new muffler had better be fixed while she thinks over how to raise the subject.

The other homeowner's problem is right next door. The neighbor's dog isn't a cute puppy anymore, and he was never properly trained. The dog snarls and leaps at the man every time he goes to rake leaves, and twice the animal has terrified the man's little girl. But perhaps the dog will grow out of it, and anyway the man doesn't want to upset the neighbors. Give the dog another chance.

The young reporter feels she did an excellent job covering the school board issue over the last six months. She's been with the paper a whole year now, yet she worries about how her boss will react to a request for a raise. She will wait until she's turned in her next article (she's pretty proud of it); it will give her the confidence she needs to speak up. Besides, there's that file to update.

These four people put things off for different reasons. They all had one thing in common though: a lack of priorities. They didn't take the time to determine what would be most important to them in the long run.

If we haven't set priorities, procrastination is easy. We just do the things we like, those that are pleasant and that interest us, and we postpone the rest. Perfectionism and fear of mistakes support the tendency to procrastinate. We may even welcome interruptions that alleviate the necessity of getting a job done right away, as they provide a convenient rationale for delay. Doing what we like first often means postponing action on things we ought to be doing. Thinking we work best under pressure justifies putting off important tasks until just before they are due. Fear of failure or of making a mistake causes us to hesitate.

When you find yourself procrastinating, consider the following:

1. Accept that there is risk involved in any decision. In many cases the sooner a decision is made, the more likely you are to gain a time advantage. Remember, too, that a timely decision allows more leeway for corrective action if it becomes necessary.

2. Establish your priorities carefully and concentrate on getting your most important task done first.

3. Schedule difficult or unpleasant tasks for specific time slots and set deadlines for their completion. Announce your deadlines to others; this additional pressure will help ensure that you meet your deadlines.

4. Develop a philosophy of mistakes. Treat them as teachers, learning from them instead of fearing their consequences. Ask yourself: "What is an acceptable result?" Then set reasonable standards rather than reaching for unattainable perfection.

5. Control interruptions and resist the temptation to drop tasks without completing them. Postpone your reward. For example, finish a task before rewarding yourself with a cup of coffee.

Indecision is the twin of procrastination. However, unlike procrastination (postponing or putting things off unnecessarily) and unlike vacillation (changing one's mind), indecision is the inability to come to a conclusion. The procrastinator says, "Well, I just haven't gotten around to it." The vacillator says, "Yes, I'd planned to go, but then I started thinking about it and right now I think I won't go." The person suffering from indecision says, "I just can't make up my mind."

Procrastination relieves us, at least temporarily, of the necessity of making a decision or taking an action. But when a decision *ought* to be made, then procrastination becomes a decision not to decide.

Indecision—the inability to make up one's mind—is a far more universal problem than was commonly thought, but it is seldom identified as such. I was surprised to learn that indecision is a trait in my own family. At first I thought it was highly unlikely that indecision could be a problem for me. After all, I've taught decision making in my leadership courses for years. Then, as I reviewed the matter with my wife, some interesting patterns emerged: I preferred making decisions jointly when others in my organization were available to participate (was I avoiding sole responsibility for decisions so that others could share the risk?), and I disliked long, written analyses when they were unaccompanied by recommendations (was I concerned that, in making my own decisions, there was only myself to blame if a decision turned out to be wrong?). Low self-image also leads to indecision when a person fears that whatever decision he or she makes may be the wrong one.

One of the highlights of my career was the opportunity to

take a decision-making course presented by Kepner Tregoe & Associates of Princeton, New Jersey. But when my boss told me he'd signed me up to take the course, I expressed surprise. I'd never thought of my decision-making ability as being impaired. When he told me the course took three days, I was shocked. "I can tell you how I make a decision in three seconds," I said. "Why do you think you're going?" was his swift response. The course opened the door to a world I didn't know existed.

I'm convinced that people are often unable to make decisions because they don't know the steps in the decision-making process. Anyone faced with a difficult decision will find that answering the following questions in the order presented will make the task of deciding much easier. These questions are adapted from the Kepner Tregoe decision-making process:

1. Precisely what must be decided? (A problem well defined is usually half solved.)

2. What are the objectives or conditions that must be fulfilled by the decision? Which are mandatory? Which are desirable or optional? What are the relative weights of the desirable objectives?

3. What are the viable alternatives?

4. What is the critical information on each alternative?

5. What are the potential negative consequences of each alternative? How serious and how likely is each of them?

6. Which is the best alternative, based on the most effective accomplishment of the objectives and the least negative consequences?

7. What steps must be taken to implement the decision,

to monitor progress, and to ensure that effective corrective action is taken when performance deviates from the plan?

Senior managers tell me that most major decisions take twice as long to make as they should. This is so primarily because people do not anticipate the problems that can arise and do not take steps to prevent them or to minimize their consequences. Once alternatives and consequences have been considered, the use of response deadlines is one way to speed up the decision-making tempo in an organization. If information from others is necessary for your decision, impose a time limit on your requests for information. State a deadline for responding. The use of response deadlines in an organization is most effective when the technique extends to the lower echelons. Anyone at any level should be encouraged to say or write, "This information is needed by ___," and to know that the response deadline will be respected.

If a person requires only approval of a request, a copy of the request can be sent to the manager with a statement such as "Unless I hear otherwise by next Wednesday, I will proceed, assuming your approval." It is, of course, wise to ensure that the approving party actually receives the unless-I-hear memo.

Remember that delaying a decision because you fear it will be wrong is often worse than making an incorrect one early, when there is still time to correct mistakes. A mediocre decision that is well implemented will almost always be better than no decision at all. By speeding the tempo of decision making, you may gain a competitive edge if the decision is right; if it isn't, you will have more time to take corrective action. "Paralysis of analysis" describes the inability to reach a final decision—the state of always wanting more facts, of always needing a "little more time to think it over." We must accept the fact that most decisions involve risks.

LEAVING TASKS UNFINISHED

It is extremely satisfying to finish a job. The student experiences satisfaction when he writes the last sentence of his history essay. The farmer is satisfied when he sees his hay stacked in the barn, the homemaker when the last window is washed, the secretary when the final page of a manuscript is typed, and the financial manager when the last column in the annual budget is balanced. Yet how often in life do we deny ourselves this satisfaction by leaving tasks unfinished?

Perhaps that's why washing dishes is a chore that a surprising number of people enjoy. It is quite clear when the task is finished. Of course, not all jobs are as clearly defined or as simple as dishwashing. But in some households, even this menial task is never entirely finished, so perhaps simplicity does not have as much to do with getting a job done as we might think. Dishes pile up in the sink and on the draining board; occasionally, one or two will be retrieved and hastily wiped for emergency use in between other half-done domestic chores. As the task mounts up and the disorder grows, an undue expenditure of energy is needed to rectify the situation; there is a continuing sense of anxiety and depression while the job remains undone.

Lest you think that the problem of leaving tasks unfinished is limited to domestic chores and leisure activities, consider the following example: Joe was asked to check some personnel forms. He had just started the job when someone phoned to ask about an overdue inventory report. He got out the inventory file but stopped to glance at the mail. A letter on the top complaining about something in the machine shop caught his eye. He dropped the inventory file, read the letter, and then started for the machine shop to discuss it. On the way he passed the cafeteria; the coffee smelled so good that he decided to interrupt his busy morning and have a cup. His day's accomplishments so far: exactly nothing.

What was Joe's problem? He lacked the "compulsion to closure," or the determination to finish the job, that characterizes successful people. As a result, he was easily distracted and he continually left tasks unfinished. If he had formulated priorities, they weren't clear. His jumping from task to task suggests he had lost sight of what he should have been concentrating on that morning.

If you have a tendency to be easily distracted—to scatter your time over a number of projects, winding up with little to show for your efforts—better planning and control of your day are in order. Take a few minutes each morning to decide which tasks are the most important ones to accomplish during the day. Tackle them one at a time. Don't let yourself be interrupted by anything else unless it has a higher priority. If you are interrupted, get back to the unfinished task as soon as possible. Don't leave it half done and start something else. People who get things done rarely let themselves be sidetracked by diversions or interruptions. They decide what comes first and stick with it until that job is completed. Then they tackle the one that's next in importance.

A very useful technique for ensuring completion of tasks is the practice of deferring rewards. How often have you said to yourself, "I'm not going for that cup of coffee until I finish this job"? Or perhaps you've said, "When this chore is finished, we're going to the beach!" Such a reward, when deferred until completion of a task at hand, concentrates your energy. It provides a dual benefit: the completed task and the special reward you earned for finishing.

Many tasks are left unfinished when an unexpected problem arises. Careful preplanning and organization allows us to anticipate such problems as not having the necessary tools or information at hand when they will be required. Thinking through a task before it is begun can save needless interruptions.

Deadlines, like deferred rewards, impose a discipline that

favors task completion. When deadlines are announced to others, additional pressure is imposed to finalize the project or task at hand. Interruptions, which will be considered in Chapter 6, should be avoided if possible. They are a primary cause of leaving tasks unfinished.

SOCIALIZING

Of course, there's always room for a little socializing in the workplace, and in every other place as well. It establishes good relations and adds zest to life. But socializing is a world-class time waster. Its world rank of nineteen is very misleading for two reasons. First, it's a major contributor to three of the top seven time wasters: telephone interruptions, drop-in visitors, and meetings. Second, as a human characteristic, it is not identified as quickly as the environmental time concerns, which we can more easily blame on someone else.

Let's look first at situations in which the personal touch can be an asset. At the beginning of a phone conversation or a sales call, a nonbusiness observation or a personal question is usually perfectly acceptable. It is generally easy to spot situations in which a little socializing can help put people at ease, but few people are experienced at limiting socializing without offending. One manager explained that he had to distinguish between keeping the lines of communication open in order to get important tidbits of information and allowing those lines to be choked by needless gossip and storytelling.

One answer lies in your written daily plan. When socializing reaches the point where you're saying to yourself, "At this rate I'll never get even my most important work done," it's time to stop the conversation or get to the point. Having a written, prioritized daily plan in front of you keeps you from getting too involved in the social scene, and enables you to extricate yourself from it, if need be. Knowing your obligations provides an ever-ready reason for departing the social scene: Simply say, "I've got a deadline to meet." Deadlines you impose on yourself are just as important, and often more so, than those imposed on you by others.

When socializing occurs because others stop by your office or desk, develop the habit of not allowing an interruption unless it is warranted. (Drop-in visitors will be discussed in Chapter 6.) Say, "Can we meet for coffee to discuss that?" Or stand up when a visitor enters and start moving toward the door when you want to indicate that the visit is over. Don't keep a guest chair for visitors to settle into.

Schedule your own socializing. If you wish to speak to someone, call to ask if he or she can have coffee or lunch with you, or suggest riding together to a meeting. Control the urge to socialize in the office. Respect others who are trying to work—don't interrupt them.

ELIMINATING HUMAN TIME BARRIERS TO SUCCESS

We've identified and partially described seven universally acknowledged human time wasters. However, each of us is an individual. Our personal time wasters may not quite fit the patterns discussed above, and the rankings we assign to them may differ from the worldwide rankings. For this reason, it is helpful to prepare a chart of your own personal time barriers. Outline the causes and solutions of each, and set a date for evaluating your progress in eliminating each barrier. A sample is shown in Table 2. Use it as a guide when preparing your own chart in Table 3.

Table 2. **Sample: Eliminating Human Time Barriers to Success**

Date	Barrier	Causes	Solutions	Date to Evaluate
1/15	1. Inability to say "no"	a. Fear of offending	Develop technique below	1/30
		b. Don't know how	Learn four steps: listen, no, reasons, alternatives	
		c. Not assessing consequences	Take log; assess time wasted in saying "yes"; take corrective action	

Table 3. Eliminating My Human Time Barriers to Success

Date	Barrier	Causes	Solutions	Date to Evaluate
	1.	a.		
		b.		
		c.		
	2.	a.		
		b.		
		c.		

CHAPTER

Breaking Managerial Time Barriers

Sound management involves the best management of time; conversely, unsound management involves poor management of time. It's logical to expect, then, that a number of our most serious time concerns would fall into the category of managerial time barriers. Three of the top five time barriers worldwide are in this category. We'll look at these three, as well as three more that rate as serious wasters of our time. Here are the managerial time barriers we will discuss in this chapter:

1. Crisis management; shifting priorities (2)
2. Lack of objectives, priorities, planning (3)
3. Ineffective delegation (5)
4. Lack of, or unclear, communication (16)
5. Lack of standards, controls, progress reports (20)
6. Not listening

Despite conventional wisdom, you will see that "managerial skills" are every bit as important in our domestic and social concerns as they are in business concerns. Very simply, this is because every home requires managing. In fact, most homes require all the skills required by most offices. Keep this principle in mind: *Don't take your work home and leave your management skills at the office.*

Taking work home has become a common practice, but an equally common practice is to leave management skills at the office. One way to measure our progress toward success is to determine the extent to which we leave our work at the office while applying our management skills at home.

CRISIS MANAGEMENT; SHIFTING PRIORITIES

How prevalent *is* crisis management, and what is it costing us in our personal and professional lives? It ranks second worldwide, according to thousands of individuals who have identified and ranked their time wasters. Most of us have experienced the feeling of suddenly realizing it's time to go home and wondering, "What *did* I get done today?" Perhaps the key staff person on a crucial project became ill and you had to get involved. Or the computer went down and data had to be gathered manually.

We are often frustrated because we don't get around to our own priorities. We feel anxious because the pendulum of unwelcome deadlines swings ever closer and we're not moving our own projects toward completion. We sense the pressure building. Our tolerance level is severely tested by others who have put us in a bind by neglecting to act or decide on time. And how often do our bosses compound the pressure by giving us more tasks than can reasonably be completed in the time allotted?

A dilemma faced by many of us deals with the conflicting

demands of work and leisure. The issue is simply, Do I work overtime to catch up and feel guilty for neglecting the family, or do I go home on time and fall further behind at work?

And what of the damage to others? In most organizations, the ripple effect of crises ranges from marked to legendary. As with tornadoes, which seem to suck everything into their vortex and spew debris across a broad landscape so that nothing in their path remains unscarred, so too with crisis management. Tension builds. Tempers flare. Important tasks are deferred. Other deadlines are imperiled. Unreasonable demands mount. Blame is directed outward.

It is not surprising that of all the time barriers, none has a more debilitating impact on the morale and effectiveness of an organization than does crisis management. Its ultimate cost, if it could be measured, would probably exceed our highest estimate.

Understanding Murphy's Laws

Murphy's three so-called laws are thought by most to be mere humorous anecdotes. Actually they have a real application to crisis management and should be taken seriously. The first, "Nothing is as simple as it seems," means that we tend to underestimate the difficulty of the tasks we face. Imagine how many battles have been lost by commanders who underestimated the opposing forces and conditions, as did Napoleon, who discovered too late the devastating force of the Russian winter. Don't underestimate the opposition or the difficulty of the task.

The first of Murphy's laws leads inescapably to the second: "Everything takes longer than you think." Not understanding the difficulty of tasks means, of course, underestimating the time required to complete them. Unrealistic deadlines will then be established. So be more realistic in your time estimates. Build in cushions to allow for the unexpected.

What happens next is capsulized in the third law: "If anything *can* go wrong, it *will.*" Practice asking "What can go wrong?" List all potential problems and prioritize them by seriousness and likelihood of occurrence. By anticipating and planning for contingencies, you will eliminate many crises and effectively control others that could not be prevented.

The failure to measure progress through regular reports, in time to take corrective action, has brought about many crises. Periodic checkpoints for such measurements should be established for all major tasks. Guard against putting off difficult or unpleasant tasks until they become crises. Establish deadlines and schedule the tasks for completion before crises can occur.

Plan for Contingencies

We define "crisis management" as reacting to problems as they arise instead of anticipating them and taking steps to prevent or limit the consequences of the most serious and likely ones. As this definition suggests, crises should be anticipated to the extent possible and steps should be taken to prevent them from happening or to limit their consequences if they do occur.

Let's imagine that a staff member who is vital to the success of your operation suddenly shows signs of being very disenchanted. As manager, you would not be apt to ignore such signs. You would take steps to identify what was bothering your employee so that it could be corrected. By identifying a problem, you might prevent the crisis that would result from unexpectedly losing a key person. At the same time, prudence dictates that you habitually cross-train employees so that when a key person is absent or departs, others can move in temporarily to help fill the gap.

Contingency planning is one of the most powerful, yet overlooked, tools for success in both business and personal life. How many times do we discover, too late, that a critical deadline cannot be met, no matter how hard we work? The tendency is to blame others. Often, the fault lies in not anticipating the potential problems more realistically or in accepting impossible deadlines. For example, service organizations such as accounting firms are noted for not questioning their clients' deadlines, even if a client might be better served in terms of quality of work by negotiating a later deadline. After implementing a time-management program, managers in one accounting firm faced a request for something "this Friday"—an impossible deadline bound to cause considerable stress and require overtime. When, with some apprehension, the accountants suggested a three-day extension to permit better results, the client immediately assented and expressed appreciation of the firm's desire to do the best possible job! Another crisis was averted.

A seldom-identified cause of crises is overreaction, or responding to a problem with more effort than the situation warrants. This can easily elevate a small problem to crisis proportions. Simple steps to counter this tendency are: (1) Ignore the transitory problem. If it will go away when left alone, then leave it alone. (2) Delegate to others problems they can handle. (3) Respond only to those crises that require your attention.

Crisis Control at Home

In our homes a number of steps are normally taken in anticipation of potential crises. Police and fire department numbers are clearly displayed on or near the telephone. Smoke detectors and fire extinguishers are in handy locations. Parents know that crises tend to increase proportionately with the number of small children; any home with small tots is a laboratory of crisis prevention. Electric outlets within reach are plugged to prevent curious children from pushing in knives and forks. Gates are placed on stairways to prevent accidental tumbles. Inviting handles of dangerous pans on hot stoves are kept out of reach, as are potential hazards like scissors and sharp knives. These are but a few of the crisis-prevention techniques that every reader benefited from as a child—and that many have used with small children of their own. It is obvious that women, who have played the greater role in raising small children, have an advantage over men in terms of background and experience for the management of crisis situations.

Consider the case of Jerrie Hurd, who discovered that living at a crisis level at home was unnecessary.* After analyzing her activities, she reached two conclusions: First, she was living at a crisis level; second, she was spending an inordinate amount of time doing things she did not enjoy. Her crisis living resulted primarily from her failure to anticipate tasks. While some tasks couldn't be predicted or deferred when they occurred, she realized that most could be organized and prioritized to provide better use of her time. She eliminated, or cut back, low-value and distasteful tasks, which made time for more important and more enjoyable things. Countering the irrefutable law that housework will fill the time available, she allocated limited time to getting it done. If something doesn't get done, it waits. To her amazement, the system has worked. What's more, the overall time spent on low-value tasks that have to be done has decreased dramatically with no noticeable change in her family's quality of life.

Elements of Crisis Control

The crucial elements for the control of crisis management can be inferred from its definition: reacting to problems as they arise instead of *anticipating* them and taking steps to *prevent* or *limit* the consequences of the most serious and

---

*Jerrie W. Hurd, "Ceasefire on Crisis Living," *The Ensign*, August 1976.

likely ones. Remember that chance favors the prepared mind. So take steps to anticipate and prevent or limit crisis situations that may adversely impact your overall effectiveness. Be prepared. Victor Hugo said, "Where no plan is laid, where the disposal of time is surrendered merely to chance, chaos soon reigns." You need not surrender your time and your life to chance, to chaos, or to crisis. The three elements mentioned above will enable you to control your crises and your time, instead of letting them control you.

Of course, lack of sound planning has long been recognized as a major cause of crises. So common is this failure to plan that it ranks third on the worldwide list of time concerns. Accordingly, we will deal with it next.

LACK OF OBJECTIVES, PRIORITIES, PLANNING

Consider the pilot who told the passengers he had good news and bad: "The bad news," he said, "is that we're lost. However, the good news is that we're making 600 miles per hour!" Most of us who fail to set clear priorities and develop sound plans to achieve them are no better off than that pilot. An examination of the worldwide list of time concerns reveals that crisis management ranks second and lack of objectives, priorities, and planning ranks third. These two, ranked as they are so near the top, no doubt affect all of us, often to a severe extent, in both our personal and our business lives.

Curiously, each has been identified as a cause of the other. The failure to plan clearly invites crises, and a crisis orientation leaves little time for planning. No other pair of time concerns, with the possible exception of telephone interruptions and drop-in visitors, ranks so consistently together and so high on the list. In my own experience, failure to plan effectively accounts for more problems than any other single managerial oversight.

In *The Time Trap* I wrote, "Nothing is easier than being busy, and nothing more difficult than being effective." Today, some 50,000 managers and 40 countries later, I can say that nothing has changed my mind. The hardest work a manager does is thinking. Perhaps this is why it's so often neglected. Bernard Baruch, the confidant of many presidents, wrote that whatever failures he had known, whatever errors he had committed, whatever follies he had witnessed in public and private life, they had all been the consequence of action without thought.

It is undoubtedly the case that some managers are in the habit of thinking only as far ahead as the end of a morning's work. While such a decision may indeed have some short-term effects, it almost certainly will have none at all in the long term. Some operations will lend themselves more readily to long-term decision making. In the lumber industry, for instance, some aspects of policy will be determined by the fifty-year period necessary to grow a mature tree. The parents of a growing family will likewise find themselves faced with long-term decisions about a new or larger home to accommodate their children and their developing interests.

Difficult as it may be to look into the future, it is absolutely imperative that we strive to do it. Perhaps Charles Hughes, one of our most knowledgeable experts in goal setting, put it best: "We can know whether what we are doing is absurd only after we have identified the goals we seek to achieve."

In 1842 Tennyson wrote:

For I dipped into the future, far as human eye could see.
Saw the Vision of the world, and all the wonder that would be:
Saw the heavens fill with commerce, argosies of magic sails,
Pilots of the purple twilight, dropping down with costly bales.

These lines from "Locksley Hall" were written long before airplanes, airlines, and a national air transportation system became reality. They are prominently displayed at United Airlines' Chicago headquarters as a constant reminder of an important belief: The future holds great promise if we think about it rather than daydream about it, if we plan to make things happen rather than wait for them to happen, if we accept rather than reject the inevitability of change. Today's leaders and innovators spend large amounts of time planning for the future instead of living in the past or relying on the present.

Reasons for Not Planning

Planning deals with the future, and the future involves risk. No one has a crystal ball to predict events with certainty. That element of risk is one many managers fear. "Who needs to guess about next year?" is a common lament. "I'm lucky if I can guess what's going to happen next week!" Indeed, planning today for future events does involve uncertainty, and that uncertainty multiplies the risk of being wrong. It also means we must commit ourselves to a course of action and be accountable if plans do go wrong. *Risk avoidance* is a common reason for failure or refusal to plan. One of the main reasons managers fail to accept team objectives is the implied accountability for the results—a responsibility most people feel more secure without. Not knowing how to plan, the lack of a simple planning system, and the fear of making a mistake in unfamiliar terrain are also common causes of not planning.

Planning is not designed to predict the future with certainty, nor is it intended to eliminate risk. It is designed to analyze the past and present for the purpose of ensuring optimum use of resources in achieving future objectives. This process does involve forecasting on the basis of the best available assumptions, where a present course will lead. It is designed to ensure that the right risks will be taken at the right time and in the right manner. One could say it was intended to reduce or control risk.

Plan for the Long Range First

"If we would only look at the cost of *not* planning," said a friend, "we'd be more prone to go through the agony." The price of not planning, of course, may be extinction. A case in point occurred in Germany. A seminar on the management process was being conducted for chief executives in Heidelberg. The publisher of the world's largest business weekly was attending. In the discussion on planning, the importance of knowing what business one is *really* in had just been emphasized. During the coffee break the publisher came to me and explained that he felt like leaving the seminar and calling a meeting of his board of directors. "Why," he exclaimed, "we think we're in the business of publishing our weekly magazine, but we're really in the communications business. We're losing money with the weekly, yet we could be making money with radio and television stations! I can't believe it! Why haven't we seen this before!"

So how do you plan? Many people say that planning their day is useless because they no sooner get started than the first crisis blows their plan right out the window. Others say that since they can't predict what's going to happen tomorrow, they couldn't possibly plan a week ahead. Some have the notion that planning the day five times over means they've planned the week; four planned weeks ought to make a pretty good month; and if they can hang twelve moderately well-planned months together, that should make a fairly well-planned year? Right?

Wrong! Planning works from long range to short, not the reverse. The reason is simple enough. If you don't know what needs to be accomplished by the end of the week, there is no way you can know what must be done today. If the goals for the month are shrouded in mystery, you can only guess about what you should have accomplished by the end of the week. And if the objectives for the year are the tightest-held secret since the company almost sold out to a major competitor, then your guess regarding the targets for the month may be no better than anyone else's. A futurist with a Ouija board would probably come as close to the truth as you would.

This is so in our personal lives as well. If we haven't determined what we must accomplish today, we can't know which task has precedence right now. Clarifying our goals has a remarkable influence on our decisions, guiding them throughout the day and the week. The homemaker who thinks only of having enough food for the dinner party may make two or three trips to the grocery store. The one who thinks also of conserving energy and time by making only one trip will make a list early and add to it as other thoughts come to mind. When the shopping trip is made, all the necessary items will have been listed and one trip will suffice. The family that is saving for a summer vacation may decide to postpone the purchase of a new car. Otherwise, when vacation time comes, the agonizing fact of insufficient funds must be faced.

Planning does pay off. I was running late as I left my office in New York for a speech in New Orleans. Jumping into the nearest cab, I asked the driver if he could get to LaGuardia Airport in thirty-five minutes. The driver didn't move. I wasn't sure that he'd heard me, and I was anxious about missing my plane, so I asked again: "Sir, do you think you can get to LaGuardia in thirty-four minutes?" Without even starting the cab, he turned slowly in his seat and said: "Mister, do you see Fifth Avenue?" "Yes," I replied, hoping my growing impatience would show, "I do see Fifth Avenue." "Mister," he continued, "do you see the parade on Fifth Avenue?" "Oh, yes, I see the parade," I muttered. "Mister," he concluded, "you'll be lucky to get past Fifth Avenue in thirty-four minutes!" Gradually, the taxi pulled away from the curb, and I chuckled. "You're laughing?" he queried with undisguised surprise. "Yes," I responded. "Where do you think I'm going and what for?" "Haven't the faintest," he responded. "Well," I continued, "I'm going to New Orleans to give a talk on time management." "No kidding," came the stunned response. "Mister," he concluded, "you're just going to have to start allowing more time."

Being a student as well as a teacher of time management doesn't mean that I don't have lapses like everyone else. I do try to learn from them and take action to try to prevent their repetition. Last-minute-itis plagues the great majority of us. It represents the most dangerous form of procrastination and, as in the case of the taxi, is a simple result of not allowing a cushion of time for whatever might go wrong.

So knowing your destination will help point you in the right direction, but it won't necessarily ensure that you get there. Planning the proper use of your resources, including time, is essential to achieve your goals. Fortunately, the plane I missed was not the last one I could catch to make the engagement. My policy is never to take the "last plane," if possible. In this case it paid off.

Analyze Your Priorities

It's one thing to have a list of "things to do." It's quite another to have a clear sense of their relative priority. I recently asked a group of trainers for their biggest problem with time. Setting priorities was named by more than half the group—it was far more prevalent than any other single problem. My surveys in seminars indicate that not one person in ten carefully prioritizes his or her tasks for the day and develops a plan for accomplishing them. I've discovered that the reason lies in not knowing how to do this. So how does one determine relative priorities among a number of tasks?

A simple method is to complete a priority matrix, as shown

in Table 4. Each task is rated according to two criteria; the resulting weights indicate the relative priorities of the tasks, with the lowest total weight equaling the highest priority. The first criterion is the long-range importance of the tasks. Over time, perhaps at the end of the year, how important will each one be? If a task is the most important one you'll be assigned all year at work, it obviously has a very high ranking in terms of long-range importance. It would be rated "1" in the priority matrix. The second criterion is short-range urgency. A task that has to be done today, regardless of its importance, would be rated "1." The lowest ranking for either of the criteria would be "3." As shown in Table 4, the combined ratings (in the "Weight" column) of each task are used to determine the tasks' priorities.

Use the blank in Table 5 to prioritize your tasks for to-

Table 4. **Sample Priority Matrix**

Task	Long-Range Importance	Short-Range Urgency	Weight	Priority
Approve A/P checks before vacation	2	1	3	2
Return job evaluation to boss	2	2	4	3
Complete proposal revisions and rush to client	1	1	2	1
Coordinate vacation plans	3	3	6	5
OK purchase of new computer	2	3	5	4

Table 5. My Priority Matrix

Task	Long-Range Importance	Short-Range Urgency	Weight	Priority
1.				
2.				
3.				
4.				
5.				

morrow. Refer to Table 4 and the instructions above as you complete the matrix.

Do First Things First

The maxim of "doing first things first" is given lip service by almost everyone. In actual practice, it's a maxim that seems to be very difficult to observe. How many times have you found yourself working on something you preferred doing when you realized that you hadn't started the really important task for the day. The urge for instant gratification prompts us to do small tasks with high appeal first. In one seminar a *Fortune* 500 group of managers analyzed their time logs for a three-day period to determine at what point in their day they began work on their number-one priority. Their answer was midafternoon! Analysis revealed a broad number of reasons for this, including:

♦ The desire to clear the desk to permit concentration

♦ The quick gratification of accomplishing small things

♦ The belief that a late start provides more thinking time

♦ The belief that we work best under pressure

♦ The belief that delaying the start delays the accounting

♦ The fear of making a mistake

♦ Uncertainty on how to begin

Catchy signs that embody a powerful principle or technique are valuable tools for people who want to be more successful. The most powerful such sign I know of reads, "Get #1 Done First." This slogan embodies three important concepts: (1) To "get . . . done" means to accomplish results, not simply to get started or stay busy; (2) "#1" indicates that your priorities are clear; (3) getting it done "first" means you've recognized the power of a deadline and have scheduled the number-one task first to ensure that it is accomplished before all others.

Pareto Revisited

Many words have been written about the Pareto principle, which states, "The significant items in a given group normally constitute a relatively small portion of the total items in the group." Surely our experience confirms that the most effective people we know don't waste time on trivia. Instead they focus on the really important, worthwhile matters. Less important things are delegated or ignored. Harry Hopkins, close advisor to President Franklin D. Roosevelt, had a heart condition that prevented him from working more than two hours a day. His intense focus on priorities led Winston Churchill to call him the most effective American he'd ever met. Churchill dubbed him "Lord Heart of the Matter."

To appreciate the Pareto principle fully, it is helpful to look at a diagram detailing its usual 20/80 aspect. As Figure 1 shows, 20 percent of all our efforts (on the "vital few") produce around 80 percent of all our results. Accordingly, 80 percent of our efforts (on the "trivial many") produce only 20 percent of our results. Finally, note that one-fourth of that 80

EFFORTS   RESULTS

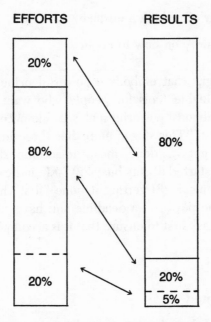

Figure 1. Adaptation of Pareto Principle

percent, or 20 percent, of our efforts on nonessentials produce only 5 percent of our total results. So the top 20 percent of efforts expended on our real priorities produce four times the results produced by the remaining 80 percent of our efforts (expended on nonpriorities) and sixteen times the 5 percent produced by the bottom 20 percent.

INEFFECTIVE DELEGATION

The word "management" first appeared in the English language late in the sixteenth century. Although today we generally identify management as an activity concerned with business and public affairs, we of course draw on management skills in many affairs apart from business. In its definitions of "management," the *Oxford English Dictionary* lists an early usage of the word: "the training, handling and schooling of a horse in its paces." The aspect of control remained central as time passed, but it was control exerted over weapons, boats, the conduct of wars, world events, and, most recently, people. Management authorities recognize the prime importance of people in the process. It's here that the skill of delegation is revealed as a major qualification of a good manager. You could almost say that a manager who fails to delegate or who delegates ineffectively is no manager at all.

The expert handling of a horse tells us something important about the delegating aspect of management. In the past the horse was an extension of the person. On a mount, and in firm control, a person could go faster, cover more ground, and perform military tactics more effectively than he or she could on foot. On the other hand, an unschooled horse could sabotage a rider's best efforts, including unsaddling him.

Although the management process involves the schooling of subordinates, a paradox exists in this area that may account for much of the frequent failure to delegate. A manager may be reluctant to delegate to inexperienced employees because she or he lacks confidence in their ability to do what is required. Here lies the paradox: By refraining from delegating because of lack of confidence, the manager denies the subordinates the opportunity to learn how to perform in a way that would justify such confidence. The answer to this quandary was identified by Saul Gellerman, the noted behaviorist. You must delegate *before* you have confidence, said Gellerman. Coach and counsel to ensure success—confidence will follow.

Although delegation will be most effective after schooling or training has been given, the benefits of the time spent on it are immeasurable and the steps are simple to learn.

How to Delegate

We may believe in the virtues of delegation and still not delegate effectively. What holds us back? There's a variety of reasons, some having to do with the sort of people we are, some with a simple lack of skill, and some with our uncertainty about what delegation is.

Let's start with the last category, as it's the simplest to deal with, and luckily, when we understand it, it's the one that can effect great changes in our management style. In effect, to delegate is to commission a person as a deputy or representative with power to transact business for another. Remember that word "power." When you give someone a job, unless you also invest that person with responsibility for it and the power or authority necessary for its execution, you have cheated him or her and foiled yourself. You haven't delegated; you've dumped! We need to remember the two-way nature of delegation. Because it's a two-way process it develops cooperation. Cooperation between two people can spread outward, as well as up and down, and become teamwork. If we don't realize that this can happen, we may stop far short of full delegation.

Next come the reasons for ineffective delegation that derive from our egos. Here, as in Chapter 4, we are up against that most intractable opponent, human nature. But once we know what we're up against, we're in a strong position.

Some people may simply prefer "doing" to "managing"; in this case, perhaps they should do exactly that and not accept a managerial role. Others may find it hard to allow someone to tackle a job in his or her own fashion or in a way they consider incorrect. If you have this problem, try this solution: Constantly remind yourself that the benefits of delegation have proved to outweigh its drawbacks and that overall you stand to gain a great deal from the practice. By allowing, even encouraging, your people to do things their own way, you will discover that they are far more motivated than you thought.

Then there are those of us who may not like to impose our will on people (though this is not what delegation should be, in any case) or to assert ourselves. We may be unwilling to take risks. We may feel insecure about our own lack of experience and thus be hesitant to delegate. But there's good news. Delegation is a skill, and if we see it this way, we can learn to use it objectively as a method of training ourselves in assertiveness. We can delegate effectively if we concentrate on *what* to delegate, *how* to delegate, and *how much* to delegate.

Last come the reasons for ineffective delegation that have to do with poor communication and organization. Often we don't make ourselves clear or bother to find out whether we have been understood. Or maybe we don't establish a system of controls to ensure feedback and to check that certain goals along the way have been met. We should work on our communication skills and give others the chance to respond. It is also important to remember that delegating is more than just assigning a task; provision must be made for receiving information and conducting progress checks as the task proceeds.

Do not mistake delegation for abdication. You as manager remain accountable for your subordinates' results.

The Benefits of Delegation

Delegation extends what *we* can do to what we can get done through others. A young woman recently became the principal of an elementary school with a pedestrian approach to children's learning. Parents regarded the school as "good" because the teachers cared about the students and kept them busy in the classroom. There were no major discipline problems, but neither was there very much excitement about education.

During her first year, the new principal realized that her teachers were her major resource. She organized them into departments so that throughout the school there was a new sharing of experience and expertise. Apprentice teachers and their classes became the responsibility of trusted older faculty members. Teachers with particular interests and skills were invited, as mentors, to direct training workshops on a weekly basis. In a few months, the principal infused in her faculty a new delight in the art of teaching, which was, of course, conveyed to the children in the form of better-thought-out and more stimulating lessons.

Delegation releases time for more important work. A single father with two school-age children divided his time among caring for his small farm, writing magazine articles, and looking after the house and the two boys. Only by training his sons in the management of the farm and its roadside stand and by giving them a share in the responsibility of running the operation, as well as in the rewards, could he secure the time he needed for the more lucrative and, to him, satisfying work of writing. This example illustrates a third benefit of delegation: It develops the subordinates' initiative, skills, knowledge, competence, and job satisfaction.

An often neglected benefit of delegation is that it allows decision making to occur at the lowest possible level at which the required information and judgment exist. This frees the manager to make decisions about long-term or priority matters that are the proper concern of top management. A man who understood the liberating power of delegation was Saxon Tate, former managing director of Canada and Dominion Sugar. While with the company, he said of himself: "I make few decisions with a time span of less than a year. At one point I made them for as short a span as one week. I now see that kind of involvement in detail as a luxury no one at the top can afford."

How Well Do You Delegate?

To see how you rate on delegation, answer the following ten questions "yes" or "no":

1. Do you regularly take work home?

2. Do you work longer hours than your subordinates do?

3. Do you spend time doing other people's work for them?

4. Is your "in" basket full when you return to the office after an absence?

5. Are you still handling any activities and problems you were involved with before your last promotion?

6. Are you often interrupted by requests for help or clarification on current projects?

7. Do you spend time on routine details that others could handle?

8. Do you like to keep a finger in every pie?

9. Do you rush to meet deadlines?

10. Are you unable to keep on top of priorities?

If you answered "no" to nine or ten of these questions, you are an excellent delegator. Even with one "yes" you would still be in this category. If you had two to five "yes" answers, you should work to improve your delegating skills. If you answered "yes" to more than five questions, you appear to have a serious problem with delegating. Place a high priority on solving it.

LACK OF, OR UNCLEAR, COMMUNICATION

How many times have you unscrambled a confused situation in which the final results bore little or no resemblance to the intended results? And how often was the search for the cause ended when someone said "But I thought you said . . ."?

Most of us take communicating for granted. Never having thought about it, we assume that people understand what we are saying and what we are trying to convey. In fact, we practically assume that our listeners are mind readers. This attitude has led many of us to respond to a comment such as "I thought you said . . ." with "But I assumed you would understand."

When we fail to make people understand us, we waste time—theirs and ours. It is internationally acknowledged that failure to communicate and communicating imprecisely are both frustrating time wasters.

We have long presumed that the drain on time caused by poor communication is easier to perceive in the corporate world than in the domestic or social world. Talk with a marriage counselor and the presumption may disappear. On the domestic scene, the most noticeable result of unclear communication is bad temper. But a look at the example below will show that the anger caused was aroused precisely by the panicky feeling that important time was being wasted.

A neighbor of mine and her husband and children had been invited out to a barbecue. They had been asked to contribute hamburger rolls and children's drinks. When her husband called from work, offering to shop on his way home, my neighbor asked him to buy the rolls and the drinks for the children. Estimating that there would be four children at the party, he arrived home with what he considered appropriate supplies. My neighbor, worried, exclaimed at the small number of rolls. She had expected her husband to provide enough for a sizable number of adults as well as the children. "But you said to bring hamburger rolls and drinks for the children," her husband protested, understandably upset. "I know I did," wailed my neighbor. "I realize that I should have said to bring hamburger rolls and children's drinks. That way you would have known I meant for you to get enough rolls for everybody, but only enough drinks for the children!" A second 10-mile trip to town to correct the error was the time cost for this minor communication failure. It's clear that this kind of mistake, in the wrong situation, would cost a business operation more than frayed tempers and half a gallon of gas.

Communication problems exist everywhere. They should always be treated as high-priority concerns. Fortunately, there are many ways to monitor and improve both social and business communications. You need energy, goodwill, and a few practical pointers.

Respect Other People's Time

Remember, time is equally important to everybody. A boss who keeps a subordinate waiting displays the same lack of respect as an employee who disregards a manager's schedule and comes late for an appointment. Successful communication requires a two-way channel and a calm context. The relationship has already begun to go wrong if one person has been kept waiting by the other. But don't make the mistake of thinking you can make up for lost time by hurried instructions. It pays to spend time on a clear message, whether it's conveyed verbally or in writing. Hastily chosen or imprecise words may end up costing much more than the five minutes it would have taken to ensure clarity.

Keep Others Informed

The office is in turmoil. Esther, the manager's secretary, received a call from a major prospective customer. She knew he would phone, because her boss had dropped a memo on her desk as he rushed out of the room an hour earlier. Unfortunately, her boss had no time to meet with her that morning to discuss the day's priorities, and the memo gave no details about what the customer would want to know. Worst of all, her boss had not said where he could be reached or when he would return. When the caller asked for information Ester didn't have, she was embarrassed and the caller was dissatisfied.

Secretaries frequently remark that their bosses don't keep them adequately informed. According to a top secretary, three most important factors in a boss-secretary relationship are (1) consideration, (2) confidence, and (3) communication. By observing a few communication rules such as those listed below, managers will improve their secretaries' effectiveness and save everyone valuable time. Secretaries summarize them as follows:

Keep us informed. (What's behind the memo? Why is a particular item important? Where are you going? When will you be back?)

Tell us what you expect.

Tell us how we are doing.

Learn to listen.

LACK OF STANDARDS, CONTROLS, PROGRESS REPORTS

Control is the most neglected of all the managerial skills. It's the managerial skill used to ensure that progress toward a goal or an objective proceeds according to plan.

It could be called the "How much do you want done and by when?" question. Deadlines, a crucial tool for anticipating and preventing crises, are a critical element in effective controls. Only when a deadline for a task or project has been determined can interim checkpoints be set to monitor progress. Putting standards and controls in place *before* they are required is a vital managerial skill. Instead of waiting to see what mistakes may occur, you establish control systems that will help all persons involved in the work perform to their highest capability. Once you have established standards and installed a system that provides for reports at regular intervals, you can be sure that deviations from the plan will be caught in time to correct them and to ensure the timely accomplishment of your goals.

As mentioned earlier, delegation without conferring responsibility and authority is just dumping. As a manager—of your own household, your own sales territory, your own theater, your own hospital department, or your own office—when you delegate, *you* remain accountable. If you are plagued by frequent questions about what you've delegated, chances are you haven't explained the job clearly. That, of course, is poor communication. But if the job doesn't get done on time, or if it is sloppy or incomplete, the cause is probably a lack of controls or interim progress reports, as well as the failure to impose definite standards and deadlines.

Too often we delegate tasks haphazardly, without thinking of how we can ensure that the work will be done well. A secure framework in the form of a detailed schedule, a mutually understood standard of achievement, and a system of self-checking on progress can make all the difference. A tangible assurance of order will inspire confidence in any individual to whom you have delegated a task. It will provide you with a convenient mechanism for recording, and checking on the progress of, tasks throughout your department, your volunteer organization, or your home. See the appendix for a description of Time Tactics, an integrated system that could be of use here.

The Importance of Deadlines

Have you ever wondered why things don't get done on time? Has it ever seemed, at work and at home, that when you give someone something to do, you can count on its not being finished when you'd like it to be? Why is it that performance is seldom up to our expectations regarding the timing of a task's completion?

Chances are the problem has something to do with deadlines—your failure to set them or to see that another person sets them, or, perhaps, to see that they are respected after they've been set. Experienced and effective supervisors and managers always think of deadlines. Inexperienced ones rarely do, except when a deadline is missed and it's time to account for what happened. Yet deadlines are crucial in establishing a system of standards and controls. Without them, progress reports would be meaningless.

Reasons for failing to set deadlines vary from not having time and not thinking about it to not wanting to put another person under additional pressure. When a task is delegated without a deadline, however, the person to whom it is assigned is unable to determine its priority, since deadlines convey priority. Tasks without deadlines cannot be taken seriously because there are so many other tasks that do have deadlines.

Picture Johnny, impatiently finishing the raking of leaves so that he can join his buddies at the swimming pool. While driving away, a parent calls out from the departing car, "Johnny, don't forget to finish cleaning the windows on the first floor." Johnny mutters, "Sure, I won't forget." What do you predict he will do when he finishes raking the leaves? Odds are that Johnny is perfectly serious and honest in his intent to remember that the windows have to be cleaned. Odds also are that when he finishes the raking, he'll head for the pool. When asked why he didn't finish the windows *before* going to the pool, he'll probably say something like "You didn't say when."

So it is at work. This scenario could be paralleled in practically any organization dozens of times a month. And the soon-as-possible syndrome doesn't help the problem. The supervisor gives a team member something to do. When asked how soon the project is needed, the supervisor replies, "As soon as possible." Time passes. The project hasn't been completed. The supervisor asks why. The team member asks, "When did you want it?" The supervisor replies that it was needed as soon as possible. "Oh," says the team member, "it hasn't been possible." The problem here, of course, is the lack of agreement on exactly what "as soon as possible" means. And this is clearly not the team member's fault; it's the supervisor's.

In both of these examples—Johnny with the windows and the team member with the project—it would have been very simple to have extracted a deadline in a few seconds. Each could have been asked the same question: "When do you think you could have it done?" Johnny might have said, "About an hour after I get back from the pool." Before accepting this as an agreed deadline, the parent might have asked, "And when will that be?" The team member at work might have said something like "How would Monday be?" In both cases a brief negotiation or a quick acceptance could take place; the deadline would no longer be in doubt and the probabilities of the task's being completed would be dramatically enhanced.

It is impossible to overemphasize the importance of setting deadlines—not only for others but for ourselves as well.

Living with Deadlines

I well remember that, as a child, I thought deadlines and threats were practically indivisible. The school bell meant we had five minutes to get to class and be in our seats. Term papers had to be in on time. We had to be home by six for supper, and we had to have the car back by eleven. The lawn had to be mowed on Saturday morning. With every deadline the threat of failure or loss of privilege was obvious.

Getting things done on time, getting everything in on time, getting to places on time—most of us become "nick-of-time experts." Salespeople must deal with making appointments and keeping them; they must make weekly quotas and turn in monthly reports, which will, sooner or later, determine whether they keep their jobs. Nine-to-fivers must arrive at work on time and face the constant pressure of completing jobs on time, whether or not the deadlines set by their bosses are reasonable.

Still, with all the pressures time limits impose, people react differently to deadlines. I can recall not worrying about the approaching tax deadline because of my accountant's usual practice of obtaining extensions. On the other hand, one young employee was worried mightily; she assumed the government could do almost anything to her, including imposing a jail sentence.

Attitudes on deadlines vary a great deal. Some people insist on always being early, while others can't seem to do anything on time. My wife sees deadlines differently than I do. She's the early bird. She prefers, for example, arriving early for a show; she allows time to find her seat and relax before it starts, instead of scurrying about at the last minute hoping to get there before the curtain goes up. On the other hand, I often delay my departure until the last minute; still hoping to arrive on time, I attempt to carve one more notch on my belt of accomplishments for the day. I tell myself, "I'll just make one more call or dictate one more letter." The first time my secretary and I listed each other's time wasters as we perceived them, I was surprised to see her number-one choice for me: "Disregards his own deadlines." I expressed surprise and told her that since they were my deadlines, I should surely have the right to disregard them if I choose to. "Of course you should," she countered, "but if you don't take them seriously, why should I?"

Some people plan their day to the minute, while others leave it entirely to chance, believing that spontaneity is an essential ingredient in life. Some people set deadlines and religiously adhere to them, punishing themselves if they miss a single one. Other people refuse to wear wristwatches so that they will have no reminder of the constraints of time. Some people consciously defy deadlines, equating the violation of a deadline to an autonomous statement of independence. William Emerson sought to dignify this last group through a bit of whimsy in his article "Punctuality Is the Thief of Time." It seems that one day while hurrying along to get to work on time, he came very close to walking into a shoot-out in which some lives were lost. He thinks that being late may have saved his life. "There's no telling how many air crashes, train wrecks and shoot-outs I've missed by being late," he mused.

Whether we honor or ignore them, most of us never think of deadlines in a positive sense. Instead, we think of the relentless pressures they cause, the ascending stress that approaching deadlines exert on us, and the sense of frustration and failure we experience by missing deadlines. Let's examine some positive benefits of deadlines to help reverse our thinking.

Overall, setting deadlines can be thought of not only as a technique for enhancing the management of our time and the quality of our lives but also as a means of reducing stress and tension both at work and at home. Four major benefits of deadlines are discussed below.

Deadlines Force You to Plan. The "hidden agenda" in setting deadlines is the fact that you must think about what has to be done and how long it should take in order to set deadlines that are realistic. Your goals must be clear before you can determine the course of action to follow: what you must do and when you must do it. Once the deadline is established for completion of a task, checkpoints can be set automatically for monitoring progress to ensure that you will meet the deadline. These factors—goals, priorities, deadlines, and progress reports—are the heart of the planning process. Without goals you can't know what to do; without priorities you can't know what to do first; without deadlines you can't know when to do it; and without progress reports you can't know how you are doing. It is clear that deadlines are an essential tool in planning both your personal life and your work life.

Announcing a Deadline Helps You Get More Done. As long as a deadline is realistic, the pressure it represents can be positive and should be welcomed. By setting and announcing a realistic deadline for accomplishing something, we increase the likelihood that it will get done. The reason for this is simple: We have been programmed since childhood to keep our promises. "Going public" by announcing a deadline is a promise to yourself and to others to get something done by a certain time.

Deadlines Help Reduce Stress. Medical authorities have established a direct relationship between stress and tension and the two top killers—cancer and heart attacks—as well as nervous breakdowns and a host of other physical ailments. The sense of anxiety and frustration generated by uncompleted tasks and missed deadlines can be eliminated by setting realistic deadlines and checkpoints. When progress lags, it will be discovered at the next checkpoint; corrective action can then be taken to ensure completion of the task or project on time. This assurance reduces the likelihood of crises and eliminates the worry, stress, and tension that almost always accompany missed deadlines.

Deadlines Provide an Inner Sense of Accomplishment. By doing what you know should be done, you are satisfying an inner need to be effective, to make a contribution, and to perform up to your highest potential. Crossing out the most important item on your daily "to do" list can provide you with a deeply satisfying sense of self-discipline and accomplishment.

SETTING AND STICKING
TO DEADLINES

While deadlines are a useful tool for getting more done in less time, few of us are as familiar with their use as we should be. Single parents who are juggling a career, home, and family face many more deadlines than others and should be even more familiar with their use and value. To make deadlines work *for* you instead of against you, some helpful tips are listed below.

1. List your goals, set priorities each day, and establish deadlines for completing them. Use these deadlines to measure your progress and to say "no" to interruptions regarding less important matters.

2. Set your own deadlines when others don't. Upon receiving an assignment or a request, ask when it is needed. Then set your own deadline, with a realistic cushion to allow for the unexpected, and do your best to honor that deadline.

3. Request that others set deadlines for tasks you give them. Ask when your request can be met, and then agree on a deadline. Be sure it is realistic for the other person as well as for your own timetable.

4. Stick with a job until you finish it. Resist all interruptions except those regarding more important matters that cannot wait. Recognize that interruptions are the most serious enemy of deadlines. When an interruption is unavoidable, return to the task immediately after the conclusion of the interruption. Remember, on average

it takes three times as long to recover from most interruptions as it does to endure them.

Monitoring Progress of Tasks

In seminars worldwide, no problem of supervisors and managers seems to be mentioned more often than the difficulty they encounter in monitoring progress on tasks they have delegated. Once the deadline has been set, checking progress becomes a fairly simple process of requiring progress reports at preset intervals. Any good time-management system will provide project sheets for plotting the deadlines for completion and the checkpoints for making interim progress reports on all delegated tasks. Ideally, a separate tab will provide a place for noting all communications with each person reporting to the manager. A project sheet should show all projects delegated to a subordinate and the current status of each.

Larry Appley, former chief executive of the American Management Association, said, "People do what you inspect, not what you expect." If you do not provide for progress reports, do yourself the favor of inspecting progress at regular intervals to be sure performance is progressing according to plan. Countless crises have been averted by alert managers who check up periodically to see that things are on track.

A valuable asset in conducting progress checks is the art of listening to what others tell you. In fact, *not* listening is such a major worldwide time waster that we will devote the next section to it.

NOT LISTENING

One manager and his secretary discovered something about one another at a communications workshop instituted by the firm. Asked to list difficulties encountered in daily affairs, both boss and secretary wrote in a prominent position on their answer sheet: "You don't listen!" They should not have been surprised. It is documented that the average adult listens effectively only 25 percent of the time. Our failure to listen well is not restricted to one area of our lives, and we often pay for this shortcoming in many ways. A universal result of imperfect listening, however, is a loss of time—time spent in smoothing out misunderstandings or, more drastically, in trying to mend broken relationships; time spent in requesting repeated instructions or explanations; in asking unnecessary questions whose answers have already been given; or in correcting mistakes caused by misunderstood instructions. Here are some behavior patterns that get in the way of good listening:

- ◆ interrupting before the speaker has finished everything he or she has to say

- ◆ allowing oneself to be distracted by extraneous sights or sounds

- ◆ sitting too far from the speaker

- ◆ judging the speaker on delivery rather than on content

- ◆ closing one's mind prematurely to the speaker's ideas

If you are in a position to do so, help people to listen well by imposing a short period of silence after the presentation of a serious problem; this gives the listeners a chance to think before they speak. This technique can be employed between a husband and wife, a parent and child, or a manager and subordinates, with positive benefits to everyone.

An obvious time to use such a technique is during a meeting. Meetings, as an environmental time waster, will be considered in the next chapter. Here we deal with a few aspects of meetings that relate to communication. Meetings, on the face of it, look like first-class opportunities for communication, and a well-run meeting may be just that. Meetings will commonly be called to coordinate activities, to exchange information to make decisions, or to build morale. All of these place a premium on effective communication.

People who are involved in only part of a meeting may be invited to attend that portion of the meeting devoted to their particular concern. The benefits of this policy are twofold. Such people will be freed to continue more useful work elsewhere, and those remaining in the meeting will find it easier to achieve effective communication if fewer people are present. An authority on the nature of meetings, Hensleigh Wedgwood, has observed: "The larger the group, the harder to establish communication among the individuals in it."* When two people try to communicate, there are two communication channels. Add a third, and you are up to six channels. When eight people are in a meeting, fifty-six possible channels of communication exist. The word "channel" suggests a final thought. The choice of the wrong channel can sabotage an otherwise good communication. Thus a conference may accomplish more than dozens of phone calls if the subject lends itself to conference format, and a single phone call can replace the circulation of an impersonal and often redundant memo.

Steps to Better Listening

Studies by Dr. Paul Rankin indicate that managers typically spend about 80 percent of their time communicating. Of this time they spend 45 percent listening, 30 percent talking, 16 percent writing, and 9 percent reading. Paradoxically, although listening is the most used skill, it is the one that is least often taught. There are many reasons why people do not listen effectively, ranging from preoccupation and lack of in-

---

* Hensleigh Wedgwood, "Fewer Camels, More Horses," *Personnel*, July–August 1967.

terest to environmental distractions and the actual words of the speaker. The art and science of listening was pioneered by Dr. Ralph Nichols, who spent a lifetime studying listening skills at the state universities of Minnesota and Iowa. Of the literature on the subject that I've read, more than 90 percent derives directly from Nichols's work. Among the steps he recommends for better listening are the following:

1. Ignore your prejudices. Listen with an open mind, and do not prejudge.

2. Avoid overstimulation. Don't overreact to emotionally charged words.

3. Listen for important points. Ignore trivia; concentrate instead on key facts that relate to main points.

4. Don't avoid difficult subjects. Make the effort required to understand them, and ask questions for clarification.

5. Take notes to reinforce understanding. Avoid trying to store excess information in your brain.

6. Avoid distractions. Concentrate.

7. Don't dismiss a subject as uninteresting. Search for helpful ideas.

8. Harness excess time (speed of thinking versus speaking) by anticipating, etc. Avoid mental excursions.

9. Ask questions.

10. Detect and interpret body language (gestures, facial expressions, etc.).

11. Read between the lines. (What wasn't said?)

12. Avoid the temptation to interrupt.

As Dr. Nichols put it, a good listener is a more efficient worker, a more thoughtful spouse, a better friend.

He tells the story of a Glenmont, New York homemaker who listened to her husband talk shop about his telephone-company job. Later she saw a trenching machine scoop a 5-foot ditch across a nearby piece of property. Because she had listened well, she knew that the machine was approaching a vital telephone cable. Her prompt warning prevented the cutting of the cable, which carried 3000 important telephone and telegraph circuits and two television channels. The telephone company rewarded her with a four-day visit to New York for her entire family.

ELIMINATING MANAGERIAL TIME BARRIERS TO SUCCESS

The managerial time barriers we've discussed in this chapter affect our productivity in everything we do—at home, at work, in volunteer organizations. There is nothing of any consequence requiring the expenditure of resources that cannot benefit by the improvement of our managerial skills; the additional time that will result can then be applied to a more successful pursuit of our goals.

To improve your own managerial skills—and eliminate your managerial time barriers—you should outline your weaknesses on a chart, as shown in Table 6. In this sample three causes have been listed for the managerial time barrier "not listening," and solutions or actions to eliminate or control each cause have been noted, along with a date on which to evaluate progress. Use this sample to complete your own chart in Table 7.

Table 6. Managerial Time Barriers to Success

Date	Barrier	Causes	Solutions	Date to Evaluate
1/15	1. Not listening	a. Preoccupation	Recognize danger of preoccupation. Clear mind and pay complete attention.	
		b. Reluctant to ask for clarification	Count cost of misunderstanding. Ask for clarification immediately if in slightest doubt.	
		c. Suspicion that you disagree with speaker	Defer judgment. Give full hearing. Weigh all facts fairly.	

Table 7. Eliminating My Managerial Time Barriers
to Success

Date	Barrier	Causes	Solutions	Date to Evaluate
	1.	a.		
		b.		
		c.		
	2.	a.		
		b.		
		c.		

CHAPTER

Breaking
Environmental Time
Barriers

Sixty interruptions a day? Impossible, wouldn't you think? Yet three of the world's outstanding time studies confirm that managers are interrupted an average of every eight minutes during the working day. Given an eight-hour day, that adds up to our startling total.

You might conclude from this that managers are more prone to interruptions than are the rest of us. If this is correct, it is obviously of primary importance for managers to examine the nature of these interruptions and to take steps to minimize them.

Of course, many of us are not managers in a technical sense. But we do have the same resources as managers do, which we must manage. And we have tasks and situations in constant need of managing. All of us have days when we feel we are at everyone's beck and call, with no time to call our own. What can we learn from the managerial predicament that we can apply to our own control of time? On a larger scale, what common elements characterize interruptions in general, and how can an awareness of these elements help us solve a universal problem?

The word "environmental" is used in this chapter in a very broad sense. It applies to any constituent of our surroundings from weather to noise level and from the clothes we wear to the schedules we keep.

The principal environmental time barriers are:

1. Telephone interruptions (1)

2. Drop-in visitors (4)

3. Meetings (7)

4. Incomplete or delayed information (13)

5. Paperwork; red tape; reading (14)

6. Understaffed; overstaffed (17)

We are certainly all aware of the vagaries of the weather. Although we may never have given a thought to its impact on our available time, a moment's consideration will suggest a multitude of ways in which the weather affects it directly or indirectly. Usually, we feel most comfortable and function most efficiently in a moderate temperature. In our own homes, we have to make certain seasonal adjustments to ensure that this is maintained. If you have ever made the mistake of waiting to replace a screen door with a pane of double glazing until the temperature dips below freezing and snow half blinds you, you'll realize that wise time management takes the weather into respectful consideration. A warning reminder on the calendar to prepare the house for winter by a prearranged date will avoid this kind of uncomfortable time wasting.

In our homes are many timesaving devices. The vacuum cleaner and washing machine have become everyday necessities. But the technology we depend on will save us time only if we keep it in good repair. A regular service contract, with dates noted on the calendar, will ensure that breakdowns are kept to a minimum.

Not many of us live in dream homes. We usually take minor inconveniences for granted, or we grumble only mildly as we climb wobbly ladders to inaccessible storage spaces or shift cumbersome furniture to accommodate guests. However, each repeated action forced on us by the environmental feature of bad design is a drain on our time. It is worth sitting down with a notebook to take stock of the advantages and inconveniences of our immediate surroundings so that we can plan to make the best use of what is available.

Most of us don't suffer from our domestic arrangements in quite the dramatic way that is described by T. H. White in his delightful story *Mistress Masham's Repose*. In the rambling country-house setting in which the book opens, the kitchen lies so far from the dining room that the cook is forced to bicycle along the stone-flagged corridors to arrive at the dinner table before the food is cold! Although our own environmental time barriers may seem relatively insignificant compared to those of the cook, it would be worth considering how we could get the better of them in some more conventional way.

Space and the way we organize and use it can save or waste time for us. If family members know where clothes, books, and writing materials are stored, they can retrieve them quickly and mornings will be free from panic and crises. There will be time for breakfast together before the day's work, and tempers will benefit. The person in charge of the household will find it useful to familiarize all family members with the storage of regularly used items. This is especially helpful in a time of emergency, such as a family member's illness or absence. The storage of household items such as linen, for example, can be organized so that sheets of different sizes are easily distinguished. The time it takes to develop such a storage scheme will be recouped later in the time the scheme saves.

TELEPHONE INTERRUPTIONS

Screening is a skill. To be sure calls are screened successfully, you must discuss telephone procedures with your assistant or secretary.* The phrase "I'm sorry, she's busy" often brings the rejoinder "Who isn't?" "She's in a meeting right now" can be a legitimate explanation, but all too often this is not the case. When a secretary is covering up for a boss, the truth is frequently discerned by the caller. The professional secretary will have worked out ahead of time a system for handling callers in such a way that the caller is not offended yet the boss's time is protected.

During periods of planned unavailability, the secretary should screen calls by asking diplomatically the name of the person calling and the purpose of the call. (Obviously, an experienced secretary will know the names and voices of VIPs and how each should be handled.) The manager should have "credentialized" the secretary by telling associates, customers, and clients the reason for screening and the problem-handling capability of the person answering the phone.

The following system has proved very effective for screening calls without offending the caller:

1. The secretary will *handle* the caller's problem if he or she can do so effectively. A division controller of a *Fortune* 500 company said, "The secretaries in the division are now handling routine matters that formerly constituted an interruption for the managers."

---

*Although I use the term "secretary" throughout, please note that the material presented applies equally to administrative assistants and any other staff members with relevant responsibilities.

2. If the problem is one that should be handled by another manager or department, the secretary will *refer* the caller to the correct person.

3. If the boss must respond, but the matter isn't urgent, the secretary will *postpone* the call. An appointment is set or a callback is arranged for a specified time. If a time is not specified, the two parties may find themselves calling each other several times before they can get through. As much information as possible should be provided to the boss for the callback.

4. The secretary will *expedite* emergency and VIP calls.

This system can be used successfully in screening not only telephone calls but also visitors and even the mail.

Dialing Your Own Calls

Should you dial your own calls? If you know that the person you are calling will probably answer and that business can be transacted without delay, the answer is "yes." However, things usually don't run so smoothly. More likely, you'll find yourself talking to a receptionist and then to a secretary—only to learn that the person you're calling is not available. On particularly frustrating days incompleted phone calls can result in more than an hour of wasted time for busy executives. Electronic improvements, including voice mail, enable one to leave a message and receive the response electronically.

Planning Your Calls

How often have you hung up the phone only to realize a few minutes later that you forgot something? This is easily remedied by planning your phone calls. Prepare a list of items to be discussed, and have relevant correspondence or files in hand when you make the call. You'll save valuable time for yourself as well as for the person you are calling. This technique is helpful whether you use the phone to place orders, plan social events or meetings, or conduct business. Be sure of your facts, and go over the reasons for your call before you dial. Jot down the points you wish to make. Then you won't have to call a second time about the same matter. Ideally, you will preserve a record of your phone conversation by incorporating your notes and your contacts' replies in the relevant section of an integrated planner-organizer such as Time Tactics. In today's litigious society, lawsuits are making detailed phone records much more important. An agency manager told me the contact logs he and an agent kept of all phone calls saved them from a million dollar lawsuit!

Coping Without a Secretary

If you share a secretary with several other managers, it may be difficult for him or her to screen all, or even many, of the phone calls. Groups of managers, such as engineering teams, tell me they love voice-mail answering machines. "When I've left a message, the ball is in their court," said one. But the answering machine must be used with restraint. There are times when we feel comfortable in the uninterrupted privacy that it affords, and we should take every advantage of that time to work undisturbed. However, we must consider the nature of our deadlines and our relationships with potential callers. The machine could be a great help to a typesetter who has a successful personally run business. Her work is largely manual, and incoming phone calls generally involve enquiries about when work can be picked up or specific instructions about new jobs or proposed changes in jobs. Switching on the machine while she works enables her to be more productive. By playing back calls after she completes a job, she has up-to-the-minute information for the next project and can postpone returning less urgent calls until a quiet time between high-pressure activities. The same advantages can be enjoyed by a man or woman working on personal projects at home and wishing to be undisturbed.

Some service industries, however, may have very short deadlines, may have customers who are inclined to change their minds about requirements, and may be highly competitive. In such businesses, if you are not readily available, customers may very well call someone else to do the work. If this is true, and if you must monitor your own calls because you work alone, you must develop your own techniques for preserving your time. Do this by establishing priorities at the beginning of each day and by vigilantly protecting them. Emphasize to your clients that their concerns will receive your wholehearted attention at the proper time. The clients will soon realize that your system is a time saver for them too.

Many people have found the answering machine to be a useful tool for protecting one's privacy in the home. It is often inconvenient to be interrupted by a call in the midst of a project. In such cases, switch on your machine and reply to calls when the project is done.

A good way to handle telephone interruptions involves using the contact or communication logs in any good organizer/ planner. They provide a record of exactly what was covered in your last conversation and what you still need to discuss, and they may also contain items you added since your last conversation. If you need to know what was decided previously, the information is right there. By keeping your written daily plan with prioritized tasks in front of you, you can more easily deflect callers when their needs are of a lower priority than tasks you are working on at the moment. When someone calls and asks for information that is not urgent, there is no need to interrupt your work. Jot the request down on the contact log, and then schedule it into one of your "handle paperwork" times on your daily plan.

Other managers without secretaries take turns screening

calls for each other. Another common technique is to use a hideaway, taking your work to a conference room or an unoccupied office where no one will be looking for you.

DROP-IN VISITORS

The four steps for screening interruptions without offending that were described above for telephone calls can also be applied to drop-in visitors. The person screening first *handles* the visitor; second, *refers* the visitor to anyone else who can handle the situation; third, *postpones* with an appointment; or fourth, *expedites* the visitor's request if he or she is a VIP or has an emergency problem.

1. When the drop-in visit is postponed to an agreed-upon time, limit the length of the meeting by setting an ending time. "How much time do you think we will need, Ms. Smith?" "Fine, then why don't we make it from 4 to 4:30?" At 4:30 p.m. Ms. Smith cannot be offended if you politely say that you have another commitment for that time. Open-ended appointments encourage socializing. A set time frame also encourages all participants to be better prepared.

2. Many managers arrange with the would-be visitor to go to their office. By going to another's office instead of meeting in your own, you maintain control because you can leave at any time.

3. Many have discovered that it's a good practice to confer standing up. When a visitor drops in, remain standing. This will prevent the visitor from settling down in a comfortable chair for a long chat.

4. Regular visits should be scheduled with those reporting to you. Each of you should keep a list of points to discuss

on your contact logs so that your time together will be productive. This eliminates the numerous interruptions that arise if contact is required whenever an item comes to mind.

The Myth of the Open Door

The theory of the "ever-open door" has dogged managers wherever it has been put into practice, which was probably never the intention of the thinkers who devised it. Decades ago, certain behavioral scientists began exploring the concept that the manager's door should be "open" to anyone with a legitimate problem. They meant that the manager's door should be open to those needing help, not standing open at all times to passersby whether they have anything important to talk about or not. Incredibly, however, the "open-door" policy has come to mean just that. The manager's door is open, presumably to enhance communication. The problem is that an open door enhances the wrong kind of communication. It encourages idle conversation with someone who may be only whiling away the time until the person next door is free.

The open door often encourages interruptions to continue nonstop all day long. The answer is simple. Close it. Redefine the word "open" to mean "accessible," which it was clearly intended to mean in the first place. Thus, "open" means open to the person who needs to see you. Anyone needing information or a decision can always get it as quickly as is necessary through the cooperation of a secretary or assistant who understands what you are trying to achieve. If callers have to knock first, the slight formality will discourage chitchat.

Unfortunately, top managements in many organizations have insisted that doors remain open to demonstrate that managers are available anytime. What they fail to recognize is that this encourages overdependence by employees and seems to solicit continual interruptions that will fragment the manager's day. No one can accomplish objectives successfully in these conditions.

Open-Office Landscaping

As if the open-door myth had not done damage enough, now we have organizations abolishing doors altogether. Open-office landscaping began nearly a decade ago. A Swedish company with a huge "bullpen" type of office that was filled with desks crowded together decided to experiment with open-office landscaping. Typewriters and adding machines had clacked and whirred continuously, making it difficult to think or concentrate. After landscaping, the area was attractively separated into sound-suppressing areas. None of the people appeared to be too closely situated. Everyone was pleased with the increased privacy, reduced noise level, and attractive surroundings.

Unfortunately, with the instant success of the original idea (without the sensitive modifications just described), the concept was soon being proposed for all other levels of management and, surprisingly, was unwittingly accepted by and large. Of course, those in favor of the idea emphasized its economics and flexibility, since movable partitions could be valuable to a growing or changing organization. They did not discuss its effects on managers, who were required to give up private offices for what many referred to as "those five-sided cubicles." The cubicles were usually smaller in size (for economy), had low partitions that could be peered over by any tall person (to facilitate air conditioning, we were told), and, most surprisingly, had no doors (for economy and easy access). The lack of doors, the promoters stated, would enhance communication. Anyone wishing to could simply walk in. They were right, communication increased dramatically. But was it the right kind of communication? Not in the opinion of the great majority of managers. Two of the most serious time wasters, drop-in visitors and socializing, were greatly encouraged.

There were conference rooms for those in need of privacy, but their inadequate numbers and the inconvenience of having to move from one's own office to discuss anything privately outweighed this supposed benefit. In fact, as many dispossessed managers have said, "If they provided as many conference rooms as are needed, there would be one per manager, in which case they would have been further ahead if they had left us in our original offices." Open-office landscaping can clearly be an improvement for any employee who formerly sat in a large bullpen with no privacy. If economy and flexibility are that important, as in the case of one state government office I visited, then open offices may be justified in limited situations. But if the ability of the management team to function effectively is a paramount concern, then these apparent benefits may be much too costly in the long run. In fact, many organizations have discovered that the ultimate costs, partly due to complicated wiring, lighting, and air-conditioning problems, far exceeded the original estimates. Understandably, under intense resistance from their management teams, some organizations have given up office landscaping, wasting, in one case, nearly three-quarters of a million dollars that was invested in the concept.

Don't Be Someone Else's Time Waster

It is easy to see that many interruptions are externally generated, that is, caused by others over whom we feel we have no control. What is more difficult to realize is that many interruptions are internal, or self-generated.

The human desire to be involved in everything and to know what's going on prompts us to chat with others. Boredom with our work or the simple desire to socialize lies behind many conversations. Most of us have never thought much about the subversive effects of our own drop-in visits. When we feel like a friendly chat, we need to remember the importance of other people's time. Be aware that you may be a nuisance, and you'll modify your habit. Don't become an environmental barrier to someone else's success.

It is interesting to note that a manager may be very good at cutting short lengthy interruptions at the office but may fail completely at doing so at home when a neighbor drops by unannounced on the weekend. Learn to guard your personal time from interruptions if you set store by what you have planned to do. If you're watching a program you care about and have arranged your schedule to see, why not tell the casual caller? If the neighbors stop by to chat on Sunday, by all means welcome them in if you have the time. But if you've arranged to meet someone else in a little while, don't keep that friend waiting merely to accommodate a drop-in visitor. There's no virtue in being patient while we watch our time being wasted. If you guard your personal time from interruptions, you'll find you have a lot more of it.

MEETINGS

Six weeks a year are lost in meetings alone. Sound incredible? Yes, but many managers call it a conservative estimate. That's the *average*! So for many the loss will be much greater. Let's see how it happens.

Your boss has called a 10 a.m. meeting with you and four of your associates in his office. As you leave your office to attend, the phone rings. The caller is an important customer, and you are delayed for ten minutes. By about 10:15 a.m. the group has assembled; as the meeting begins, your boss's secretary buzzes to say the organization's president is calling your boss. You and your colleagues wait while a few apparently routine questions are answered. When the session finally gets underway, there is something the boss wants to discuss. You were not informed of the topic ahead of time, and there is no agenda. After a few minutes the original subject is bypassed and the focus shifts to a new problem. You and two of the others have no interest in the new subject. You begin to think about your desk, your unfinished tasks, and the urgent matters awaiting your action. Sound familiar? "All too familiar," say managers and meeting attendees whenever I have asked them.

You may question the inclusion of "meetings" in the "environmental" classification, but meetings have become part of our surroundings! The average manager spends two hours a day in meetings. Surveys show that 90 percent of managers worldwide say half that time is wasted. This represents an average of one hour lost each day, or six weeks of working time each year. Most managers do not cite their own meetings as time wasters, but believe they waste time in meetings called by others. One Vancouver organization's president was grateful for the insight this revelation brought. Head of a 5000-person organization, he had been meeting daily with his top ten people for approximately an hour and a half, without an agenda. They typically spent the first half of the meeting trying to decide whether they had anything to talk about; the last half was usually spent disagreeing, since no one had come prepared. Decisions were a rarity. After a company seminar on time management, the president cut these meetings to one hour weekly, with planned agendas and minutes immediately following. The consensus of his management team was that their results doubled in approximately 15 percent of the time previously spent. The productivity improvement in these meetings exceeded 1000 percent:

$$\text{Productivity} = \text{results/time} = 200/.15 = 1333\%$$

How to Save Six Weeks a Year

Implementation of the suggestions below will help you eliminate meetings that are time wasters and enable you to achieve more—in less time—at meetings that are necessary.

Unless Absolutely Necessary, Don't Call Meetings and Don't Attend Them. To adhere to this rule, you've got to be clear about why meetings are called so that you can choose alternatives to meetings when possible. A surprisingly common but rarely identified cause of excessive meetings is the reluctance to take individual responsibility for a decision. A meeting is a convenient but very ineffective process for turning an individual decision into a group discussion. Inadequate preparation, weak leadership, and failure to follow up on decisions contribute to this degradation of an important managerial tool. ' A telephone call or two may be an alternative if consultation is necessary. Conference calls regularly save travel time and expense. Instead of attending a meeting, you might send a representative. Meetings can sometimes be consolidated so that agendas can be combined.

Don't Meet if There's No Clear Purpose. Before you call a meeting, compile an agenda for it. How can you know if a meeting is necessary if you don't know what you want to accomplish? Is it to analyze, to decide, to inform, to coordinate, to brainstorm alternatives? An agenda with a stated purpose should be distributed, preferably well ahead of time, to ensure that participants come prepared. Successful control of meetings requires a clear purpose and agenda even for a meeting between two people.

A division controller of an international company told me that this practice has saved him many hours each week. All appointments are made through his secretary, who learns the purpose of the proposed meeting, negotiates the amount of time that will be necessary, and obtains as much information as possible regarding the subject to be discussed. The controller then has all the background information he requires. With a specific amount of time agreed upon for the meeting, he has found that his team members arrive much better prepared than previously.

Limit Your Attendance at All Meetings. When possible, attend only for the length of time you need to make your contribution. A personnel director in a *Fortune* 500 company saved two hours a day by observing this practice. When someone called to invite her to a meeting, her secretary would inquire whether it would be possible for the director to make a contribution at the beginning and then leave or to arrive toward the end of the meeting. The secretary would explain that the director was having a very busy day and would appreciate limiting her attendance to the time required for her contribution. Previously, this director had averaged more than four hours a day in meetings. After implementing this practice, her average time in meetings dropped two hours a day. This daily savings represented three months of work time per year!

Avoid Rescheduling. Check the calendars of all participants before setting a definite date and time. Ask each to place a "hold" on the desired time. Then notify each of the confirmed date by sending the agenda. If a participant must cancel because of an emergency, ask the person to send a representative or to give his or her contribution in writing or over the phone. Frequently, participants do not realize the importance of a proposed meeting or the inconvenience and time lost by cancellation. One secretary spent three hours rescheduling a meeting that her boss had canceled without giving any thought to the consequences.

Stick to Your Agenda. Begin and end all meetings on time. When a meeting starts late, those who arrive on time are penalized while latecomers are rewarded. Those who came on time tend to arrive late for the next meeting because experience has indicated that little importance is attached to promptness. Further, latecomers who were rewarded tend to come even later the next time. A time-limited agenda will keep the meeting on track and ensure that it ends on time. A specified amount of time is allotted to each subject according to relative priority. At the end of the allowed time, decisions are summarized and recorded before the next subject is considered. If there is digression, the chairperson might say: "Those ideas are excellent. Perhaps we can discuss them at the next meeting. However, if we are to complete our objective for this meeting, we must adhere to the agenda."

Select the Right Place for the Meeting. Interruptions can destroy meeting effectiveness. Select a site where interruptions can be avoided, and obtain agreement that no phone calls, other than emergencies, will be permitted. Every needless interruption wastes the time of everyone in a meeting. Callbacks can be taken and returned at a specified time. Ask yourself if there are any problems that cannot wait until the meeting is over. You will usually find there are none.

Keep Minutes. Decisions should be summarized. Responsibility for follow-up action, with deadlines, should be assigned and monitored. Within forty-eight hours of the meeting, minutes should be available for each participant and any outsiders with a need to know. If detailed minutes are not necessary, develop a format in a system such as Time Tactics. Those responsible for carrying out the decisions should provide progress reports at predetermined intervals on actions taken.

Evaluate Your Meetings. How did it go? Was the advance information adequate? Was the agenda adhered to? Was the objective or purpose achieved? Answers to such questions will help you streamline your meetings and ensure their productivity.

Getting More from Meetings

The following outline provides twenty-one rules that will improve both the efficiency and the productivity of your meetings.

BEFORE MEETING

1. Generate alternatives (arrive at decision, hold conference call, postpone, cancel, or send a representative).

2. Define the purpose clearly (to analyze, decide, inform, coordinate).

3. Limit attendance (only persons needed should attend).

4. Stagger attendance (attend only for the time needed to make contribution).

5. Pick the right time (strategic timing: availability of information, people, etc.).

6. Pick the right place (remote, to avoid interruptions, but accessible).

7. Send an advance agenda and information (no surprises; all participants prepared).

8. Compute the cost per minute (cost of starting late and of topic discussion).

9. Limit the time spent on each agenda topic (apportion time according to importance).

10. Limit the length of the meeting (establish and advise starting/ending time).

DURING MEETING

11. Start on time (don't penalize those arriving on time and reward latecomers by waiting for them).

12. Assign timekeeping and minutes responsibility.

13. When the agenda is short, hold a "stand-up" meeting.

14. Start with and stick to an agenda (style of leadership for the chairperson may vary depending upon the purpose of the meeting—to inform, generate creative solutions, or decide).

15. Prevent interruptions (no phone calls or messages other than emergencies).

16. At the close, summarize the meeting (state whether the purpose has been accomplished, restate conclusions, and clarify assignments).

17. End on time (respect the plans of participants who assumed the meeting would start/end on time).

18. Evaluate the meeting (was advance information adequate; did the meeting start on time; was the agenda followed and purpose achieved within the time allocated; were the right people in attendance; was time wasted?).

AFTER MEETING

19. Expedite the minutes (include any decisions, names of persons responsible, and deadlines; distribute within forty-eight hours).

20. Follow up (progress reports, execution of decisions).

21. Take inventory of meetings called and attended; use this information to improve performance.

INCOMPLETE OR DELAYED INFORMATION

Incomplete, inaccurate, and delayed information constitutes another kind of interruption to your work flow. Remember this when you frame your requests for information: Be precise about what you need; if appropriate, indicate briefly why you need it. This will encourage a more sympathetic and informed response from your source. And always give a deadline so that your request will be taken seriously. Assertiveness pays here.

A common problem with ensuring timely and reliable information is the lack of a system. Follow these straightforward rules to get over this difficulty:

1. Schedule your project so that you can see at a glance when you'll need the components.

2. Provide a cushion of time against possible delays.

3. Get your requests for information out soon enough for them to be responded to.

4. Set a precise deadline for the receipt of information.

5. Never ask for anything "as soon as possible"!

6. If appropriate, accompany your request with an "Unless I hear from you . . ." memo to verify agreement with your own decisions and deadlines.

7. When you ask for a callback, leave a message about the subject to prepare your caller. This often saves a second call.

8. Note on your calendar the dates on which you intend to follow up on the progress of your request.

9. Check your calendar and make appropriate checks.

When you yourself are asked for information, your efficiency becomes a factor in someone else's management of time. In a sense, you become part of their "environment." Take the time to gather all the information you need, and inform the requesting party about any problems you foresee. If your boss asks you for "sales for last month," you should ascertain immediately what the figures will be used for. Does he or she want the figures organized by product, salesperson, or client? By day, week, or month? And, if you're going to pull that information, does your boss need any other information that could be pulled at the same time?

If you have a deadline for providing information, and you know you won't have the data ready on time, notify the person who requested it. Ask your sources to do the same when you request something. This will save time for all concerned.

PAPERWORK; RED TAPE; READING

"Paper Jam"! These warning words light up on many copy machines when the mechanism is clogged with paper. They ought to light up in our heads when our lives at home or at work become choked in the same way. Paperwork, red tape, and reading rank fourteenth as a time waster worldwide.

Minimizing Paperwork

The problem of excessive paperwork is not an isolated one. It is worldwide in scope. My investigations in forty countries reveal that thousands have surrendered control over their jobs to random notes, memos on urgent requests, reminders of impending deadlines, and calls waiting to be returned. They are haunted by a trail of unfinished tasks, and they feel guilty even thinking about leaving work on time. Even those who have tried to solve the problem find that within a few days they have fallen back into their old bad habits.

The electronic age has made computers, calculators, and other sophisticated equipment a common sight at home and in the workplace, but these electronic marvels do not necessarily minimize paperwork. Indeed, they sometimes result in its proliferation. Documents, reports, and memoranda may be spewed forth in unnecessary profusion unless we make these machines our servants, not our masters. "Memoitis" can't be blamed on machines. They do not initiate memos. If you find memos littering your life, take steps. Memos have four distinct uses: to advise, to remind, to clarify, or to confirm. If that's not what they do, scrap them. And always ask yourself before you write one whether a phone call would serve better. Remember, using memos to communicate is a one-way system at best. Their danger is that they may be misread, or not read, or even seen by the intended recipient.

People, not machines, generate long reports and documents. These often go unread or are only partially read. They may waste both the writer's and the reader's time. Subject such documents to severe scrutiny at the conceptual stage. Don't write a long report unless one is specifically requested. And don't send out regular reports without checking periodically to see whether recipients still need them. If they don't, save the paper *and* the time.

Once you finish a piece of paperwork that accomplishes your objective, don't hang on to it, hoping to perfect it in a final draft. Send it on its way. Spending another hour on it probably won't improve it much. Perfectionism is the enemy of time control.

Don't hoard papers. Decide what to do with them swiftly, and handle them once and for all. Don't overload your files with documents of temporary value. An organizer such as Time Tactics can serve as an adjunct to a filing system, permitting you to store required short-term information in a convenient way so that it is instantly accessible.

Trust yourself and your secretary or assistant if you have one. Statistics show that 69 percent of all executives reread letters before they are mailed. What a duplication of effort! You should have absolute confidence in your secretary's accuracy.

You will reap many benefits by keeping your desktop cleared. The psychological value of seeing the top uncluttered is considerable. If you have a secretary, give him or her the permanent responsibility of removing extraneous papers and other items. Show that you appreciate the job your secretary does. In the process he or she will learn which things are important and where everything is kept. If you need a rationale for banishing the stacked desk from your life, listen to a former chief executive of General Electric, Ralph Cordiner: "Isn't one thing important enough to be done at a time? It makes it easier to finish one task without being interrupted by another." Once your desktop is cleared, keep on the desk only the job at hand. All other paperwork must wait, in its place, until you need it. Take all possible action on the current job before disposing of it once and for all.

Institute for yourself, or have your secretary set up, a color-coded system for handling all your paperwork. Suggested categories are "Urgent," "Dictate," "To Do," "Review," "File," and "Discard."

Learn the importance of a strategically placed wastebasket. All paper is not of equal value. (That goes for your own written thoughts and those of others.) Send the paperwork on its way when you have finished with it, and begin working on your next priority.

Handling Mail. We are all beset by mail. "Junk mail" builds up on our tables and shelves even though it should often be immediately consigned to the wastebasket. Other mail, such as tax forms and bills, will not excite us but demands response. We must fend off this sort of paper blockade with a uniform handling plan.

Although the volume of mail won't be as great in a home

as in a business, it's a good idea to designate a special time for opening and responding to mail. This paperwork need not interrupt our hours of highest energy—for instance, if we like to use our peak morning hours to clean the house or work in the garden, we can save opening letters for a quiet afternoon time. Applying the same sound principle in the workplace, a manager may ask his/her secretary to handle mail during a slack hour, perhaps just after lunch. Wise delegation will ensure that the secretary screens all mail and is authorized to act upon it immediately wherever appropriate. Five procedural steps expedite this job:

1. Discard, if appropriate.

2. Deal with mail on a priority basis, acting upon all items that can be handled immediately.

3. Mark items for referral to appropriate person.

4. Place in follow-up file for handling at future date.

5. Decide which items should be reviewed by the manager and prioritize accordingly.

As a check on your inclination to attach undue importance to any item that arrives by mail, consider the tongue-in-cheek advice of the manager who regularly allowed mail to "mature" for three months: If, when you finally open it, an item is still pertinent, send a response! This would be a more radical approach than most of us would care to take, but it might make us reconsider our priorities.

One of the anxieties of a prolonged trip away from home or office is the backlog of unanswered letters on your return. A friend solves the problem this way. Both he and his secretary carry a portable recorder and a supply of blank tapes. After lunch every day she opens her absent boss's mail, reroutes items within the office as necessary, and then makes a recorded summary of the most important correspondence. She mails the tapes to her boss, who listens to them the next day and dictates abbreviated responses. The secretary compiles replies from the notes and mails them out the same evening. Two days after the arrival of the letters, answers are on the way. The increasing proliferation of lap-top computers, facsimile machines and electronic mail will further speed this facsimile machines will further speed this process.

All the timesaving suggestions in the world are useless until you take the time to put them into action. Set aside time not only for catching up on unfinished work but for implementing new and more efficient procedures.

Read More Efficiently

The way we read can affect the success of our organization and our personal lives. Reading demands concentration and takes time. We can read while we travel, eat, or wait for appointments but not while we perform other activities that take all our attention.

We often read more than we need to, and we often read more slowly than we might. In some operations employees spend as much as 30 percent of their time reading. If this could be cut, across the board, much time would obviously be saved and much potential energy would be released for productive work. All individuals who read as a function of their job or special interest should maximize their speed. You might consider a speed-reading course. You can double your reading speed and improve comprehension at the same time. Managers should look into opportunities for their staffs to do the same.

In addition to increasing your speed, you should take steps to cut down on the amount you read. When reading for informational purposes, always practice techniques that will minimize the material you must read. Scan the table of contents to get an idea of the topics a magazine or a book covers, and then read closely only relevant chapters or pages. Adhesive Post-its can be used to call attention to sections that you intend to read or refer to later.

If you head a team or run a group, make it a habit to circulate important material to interested members. Attach a routing list, allowing two days a person. As manager, place your name last. You will derive several benefits from doing so. Your subordinates or the other team members will note important items and possible applications of the material, which will give you an insight into what they consider to be significant. You will get to know them better. And you will not need to read as much. You may sometimes find that you will not need to read the document at all. If the routing produces no comments or questions, consider canceling your firm's subscription to the publication.

UNDERSTAFFED; OVERSTAFFED

Overstaffing may not be a familiar problem to the reader. Yet in any organization in a fast-changing world, some business units become redundant or outmoded as fast as new ones are developed. Avoiding the problem of superfluous staff in the midst of constant change is indeed difficult. It is not unusual to discover that one element of an organization, even a small one, is overstaffed at the same time that another is understaffed. Thus, matching staff size to a company's needs is one of the great problems of growth and, indeed, survival.

The problems of overstaffing are rarely vocalized. How many managers have you known who have complained about having too many people reporting to them? The human instinct to "empire-build" makes this difficult. Office politics centers as much on extending responsibilities and building staff as it does on any other factor.

Alternatively, faced with an apparent lack of staff, how does one demonstrate the need for additional workers? By doing a cost-benefit analysis. Keep time logs, and identify every task a proposed additional worker could have done. Calculate the value of those tasks, and compare that value to the cost of hiring the additional worker. Also show any spill-over benefits that would accrue, such as new tasks you could take on if some of your old ones are delegated to the additional worker. Often, two or three managers or supervisors will combine time logs to demonstrate how a part-time employee could help each of them.

I once worked for a company in which this use of cost-benefit analysis was policy. When, for the third time, I asked for an assistant, the vice president of personnel of the parent organization, whose approval would be required for the additional staff, told me I'd never get an assistant if I continued going about it the way I was. He said that if everyone who'd asked for additional workers had been given them without a cost-benefit analysis, the company would have gone out of business long ago.

Time management plays an important part in the apparently understaffed situation. The average manager wastes two hours each day; as noted earlier, that's three months of work time in a year. Suppose that the supervisors of such managers were also wasting two or more hours a day, which is easily demonstrable from time logs. Effective time management could mean adding three months of work time for every supervisor or manager in the organization. For every four such people, theoretically, one full-time worker would have to be added to the work force. So the best answer to being understaffed is effective time management for the entire organization.

The Quiet Hour

The need for uninterrupted times for quiet concentration has been recognized by everyone. For more than a decade managers have been implementing *quiet hours*—set periods of time free from interruptions. My surveys show that a person gets three hours of normal work done in one uninterrupted hour. That's a savings of three months of work time each year! Homemakers who hold jobs outside the home also practice the same technique. One hour of peace and quiet in the bedroom, shielded from the demands of children and spouses, can soothe shattered nerves and put a smile on your face. There are some cautions. One executive who came to me for help was inundated with paperwork that only he could handle. The mountain on his desk grew ever higher, adding even more stress to his already busy day. I suggested a daily quiet hour, during which his secretary would screen callers and visitors and take messages for callbacks at specified times if necessary.

"Not on your life," responded the executive. "An associate of mine took a quiet hour to catch up and a client in charge of a half-million-dollar account called. The secretary told this client that her boss was taking a quiet hour. 'A quiet what?' demanded the offended client, and he hung up."

You might conclude that the only solution would be to fire the secretary, but perhaps the secretary had never been given a list of the VIPs with whom the boss would speak at any time. Also, the outcome might have been different had the manager told his client: "I want you to know that constant, low-priority interruptions are preventing me from having the time I would like to handle your account. I've asked my secretary to screen calls and visitors from 9 to 10 each morning and to give me callbacks at 10 a.m. However, I have given her your name and instructed her to put you through immediately if you wish to call during that period." There is a strong possibility that the client would avoid calling unless necessary.

Mark R. Ungerer, president of the Flexcon Company in Massachusetts, says the quiet hour works this way in his organization: "Our quiet hour runs from 8 to 9 a.m. when we are on normal hours and from 7:30 to 8:30 a.m. when we are on summer hours (June through August). Most of the people close their doors; those in open-office areas have small tent signs which they display. All of us, when we are interrupted, will politely tell one another, 'You're ruining my quiet hour.' It really works!

"As with any change, we had our share of 'doubting Thomases,' but once everyone knew that the quiet hour was *not* optional, it became a very selfishly guarded time. I personally monitor from time to time and make no bones about the fact that there are no exceptions.

"Most people at Flexcon would agree that the quiet hour results in accomplishing at least two hours of work in one . . . some of us will say three . . . all of us would complain if the quiet hour was taken away!"

An accounting firm in Alaska has gone a step further. Kristy K. Humphrey of W. M. Burnett & Associates, wrote us that in order to help accountants accomplish their work in the "off season" (June 17 to December 31) the following schedule is used: "The accountants work behind closed doors from 8 to 11 a.m. During this 'work break,' as we call it, they receive no phone calls, appointments, or drop-in visitors. The receptionist takes messages . . . and delivers them . . . at 11 a.m. The accountants use the next hour for returning their phone calls. After lunch, at 1:30 p.m., they receive drop-ins, calls, and appointments. Once our clients were oriented to our new schedule, they cooperated by calling mostly in the afternoons. As a result, the mornings are relatively quiet and even the receptionist is able to get a lot accomplished. After adopting these procedures, we found that our production increased, morale improved, and all concerned were much more relaxed."

Several conclusions are possible from experiences to date regarding the rapidly growing practice of the quiet hour. For best results:

1. The practice should be organizationwide, if possible. This will reduce the number of people trying to interrupt others during the quiet hour—and possibly being offended if they fail.

2. All should be observing the quiet hour at the same time to avoid encouraging the interruption of other people's quiet hour.

3. The earlier in the morning that the quiet hour is held, the better; it should occur before normal telephone, visitor, and meeting traffic reaches full speed.

ELIMINATING ENVIRONMENTAL TIME BARRIERS TO SUCCESS

To help eliminate your environmental time barriers, you should outline your weaknesses on a chart, as shown in Table 8. In this sample three causes have been listed for the environmental time barrier incomplete or delayed information, and solutions or actions to eliminate or control each cause have been noted, along with a date on which to evaluate progress. Use this sample to complete your own chart in Table 9.

Table 8. Sample: Eliminating Environmental Time Barriers to Success

Date	Barrier	Causes	Solutions	Date to Evaluate
1/15	1. Incomplete or delayed information	a. Lack system	Determine information necessary; arrange to obtain on systematic basis.	1/30
		b. Not testing reliability	Test reliability	
		c. Not anticipating delays	Anticipate and correct	

Table 9. **Eliminating My Environmental Time Barriers to Success**

Date	Barrier	Causes	Solutions	Date to Evaluate
	1.	a.		
		b.		
		c.		
	2.	a.		
		b.		
		c.		

C H A P T E R

Goals and Time—
The Keys to Success

Lloyd Loffet brought more insurance agents to the prestigious Million Dollar Round Table than any other person in his time. A year or so before his death, I asked him to draw on his broad experience in coaching successful agents and tell me which factors he considered to be the key elements in their success. He thought a moment and replied: "Goals and time. If you don't manage your time you'll never achieve your goals. But if you don't have goals, you don't need time because you aren't going anywhere. Top goal achievers are always top time managers."

Dick Brunsman came to the same conclusion, by a slightly different route. Dick, a top agent for New York Life, was puzzling over why some of the agents who come to hear him speak don't seem nearly as interested as most in learning how to manage their time better. Dick discovered that those who were not interested in time had no goals. No wonder they didn't need more time! Since they had no goals, as Lloyd Loffet put it, they weren't going anywhere. Their attitude suggested, "Wherever my efforts take me is okay." That makes life easy, if that's what you want.

WHAT DO "GOAL GETTERS" DO?

The following list highlights the key elements in the goal getter's approach to life:

1. Goal getters know that successful people set and achieve optimum goals, so they set the highest goals they believe they are capable of achieving given the resources at their disposal.

2. They focus on optimizing their resources, managing effectively, and achieving their goals.

3. They have a written plan for achieving their goals on a yearly, monthly, weekly, and daily basis.

4. They know the cost of personal disorganization, so they practice the art of getting and staying organized. By practicing sound time-management techniques, they save two hours a day or three months of working time a year and convert that time to improving personal productivity.

5. They recognize the vital importance of having competent staff.

6. They recognize that they are susceptible to the do-it-yourself syndrome, so they do nothing they can delegate.

7. They motivate their staff members by making them part of their team, including them in goal setting, and keeping them informed.

8. They continually monitor progress toward goals—daily, weekly, and monthly. They review and revise their

strategy to conform progress to goals. They keep their goals visible so that the objectives will not be forgotten.

9. They make timely decisions, set deadlines, and start early to avoid procrastination. Goal getters get number one done first in order to double their productivity.

10. They know that communication is the glue that holds an organization together. They practice it with their prospects, clients, and staffs. They learn to listen and to understand nonverbal communication.

In sum, goal getters are successful managers of their time, their tasks, and their goals.

DEVELOPING GOAL-GETTING HABITS

Self-management, which is what time management really is all about, involves habits. We are told that 95 percent of all our actions are the result of habit rather than of conscious thought. That is just as well, for imagine the time we would otherwise spend in deliberating over all the things we do naturally and habitually. William James, the great nineteenth-century anatomist turned psychologist, pointed out the advantages of habit in the smooth functioning of society. By depicting the wretchedness of a man for whom every act required a conscious choice, James emphasized the virtue of habit:

There is no more miserable person than one in whom nothing is habitual but indecision, and for whom the lighting of every cigar, the drinking of every cup, the time of rising and going to bed every day, and the beginning of every bit of work, are subjects of deliberation. Half the time of such a man goes to deciding or regretting matters which ought to be so ingrained in him as practically not to exist for his consciousness at all.

It is obvious that the habits we need to practice for sound management must be good habits and that these must take the place of bad or slovenly habits we may have developed over the years. This is not an easy change to make, as anyone who has ever tried to stop smoking, overeating, being late, or forgetting will confirm.

Listen again to the advice of William James on the importance of the formation of sound habits. He called habit:

> . . . the flywheel of society, its most precious conserving agent. The great thing is to make the nervous system our ally instead of our enemy. We must automate and habituate, as early as possible, as many useful actions as we can and guard against growing into ways that are disadvantageous as we guard against the plague. The more of the details of our daily life we can hand over to the effortless custody of automatism the more our higher powers of the mind will be set free for their proper work.

Replacing an old bad habit with a new sound one is a tall order. Fortunately, as with so many other apparently insuperable tasks, the experience of others teaches us that we can follow some relatively simple steps to success. We will need willpower and perseverance on top of know-how.

Here are six steps to help you progress from an old bad habit to a new good one:

1. *Recognize the difficulty.* Bad habits of a lifetime aren't broken easily.

2. *Develop a better way.* The best defense is a good offense. The easiest way to break a habit is to replace it with a better one.

3. *Launch the new habit strongly.* Weak initiatives die quickly.

4. *Go public.* By announcing your intention, you will be committed. If you solicit the assistance of others, they will help.

5. *Repeat it often.* Take every opportunity to practice the new habit and reinforce it.

6. *Allow no exceptions.* Exceptions quickly become the rule, and you'll be back to your old bad habit.

To change one's behavior there are really three bases to be touched. They are:

1. Knowledge

2. Attitude

3. Action

The toughest part of the process is the action plan. It's tough because the plan requires that you develop a new behavior. Specialists who study the process of habit formation have observed that it takes twenty to thirty days of continuous repetitive action to "set" a new behavior. Even with determination and a clear objective that's a tough challenge. It helps to have a companion along the way. That's what this final chapter aims to provide.

If you've followed through the book systematically to this point, you'll recall that Chapters 1, 2, and 3 explained why sound goals and well-managed time are the keys to achieving success. Chapters 4, 5, and 6 provided practical suggestions for eliminating three broad categories of time concerns: human, managerial, and environmental time barriers. These chapters should gain two hours a day for anyone who seriously applies their concepts and techniques. This chapter contains an overview of the tools that can be used in building an action plan.

MANAGING YOUR PERSONAL TIME WITH YOUR FAMILY

You will want to expand your action plan to include every aspect of your life. Although time-management studies began by focusing on the workplace, there is now increasing awareness that time-management concepts effective in business can be equally important in the management of one's leisure, personal, and family time. We should demonstrate the same concern for the quality of our personal lives as we do for that of our work lives. Here's an example of a personal application that most families will recognize.

Weekends never seem long enough for everything a family wants to do. And as children reach their teens and develop interests of their own, demands on parents' time are often bewildering, especially until the children are old enough to go places on their own. Every weekend a conflict is likely to arise in even the most well-adjusted household. For example, you may have to say "no" to an eager request from a son or daughter because you made a promise to a friend or have household responsibilities that have to be fulfilled. An emotional scene flares up. You feel guilty and angry; your children see you as unfeeling and autocratic. No one enjoys the weekend. The inelasticity of time seems to be at fault here.

On a flight from Phoenix to Chicago, I compared notes on this sort of problem with a young businesswoman who recognized herself and her family in my description. She described rather vividly a particular situation that had occurred in her family just as her elder son, Ted, turned 14. Ted had an avid interest in flying, and his heart was set on spending every weekend at the local airport, about 20 miles from home.

Of course, he could not drive himself, and no public transport existed. He had a busy school schedule and a heavy homework load even on weekends. He worked pretty hard every day at school and, like all teenagers, needed a fair amount of sleep. This is the way Ted viewed his priorities for one particular weekend:

Must do homework before Monday.

Absolutely must get to airport at crack of dawn on Sunday morning.

Want to stay in bed till last moment before we leave.

Ted's father, who ran his own type shop, also kept a small dairy farm and milked his flock of goats every morning. On the weekend in question, the family had a houseguest who had expressed the desire to attend 8 o'clock mass on Sunday in a church a half dozen miles away. So the father's mental picture of his priorities for that weekend looked like this:

Must do milking and other associated chores.

Then must drive Harry to mass; leave by 7:40 a.m.

Want to get Ted to airport, but don't see how it can be done. (Anyhow, he's got all that homework.)

Growing interested in the problem, the woman and I applied our time-management techniques to her family problem. We came up with the framework shown in Table 10.

What has happened here? First, Ted and his father have clarified for themselves the difference between priorities and preferences. Then each has accommodated himself to the needs of the other in such a way that everything they both wished to do and had to do could be accomplished in an orderly, timely way.

When we work with other people in our jobs or in our

personal lives, we are at least in some ways part of a team. Our goals are common, we may have individual responsibilities, but we rely on one another for support and resources.

Table 10. Family Priority Resolver

Person	Priority	Preference
Stage A		
Father	1. Do milking and chores.	
	2. Drive friend to mass.	
		Transport son Ted to airport.
Ted	1. Get to airport early Sunday.	
	2. Finish homework by Monday.	
		Sleep late.
Stage B		
Father	1. Do milking.	
	2. Drive friend to mass.	
	3. Drive Ted to airport after breakfast?	
Ted	1. Complete homework on Friday and Saturday.	
	2. Get up early and do all chores but milking.	

MANAGING TIME WITH YOUR TEAM

For time management to work successfully at home or in an organization, all the "team members" must work together. As in any team, members have different functions as well as individual needs, strengths, and weaknesses. There will be the need for a boss and/or a coordinator; these roles don't always have to be filled by the same person. In a family, the husband and wife may work together, or they may divide the responsibility between them. It's important that the coordinator be organized, since a disorganized manager can cause time-wasting problems for a team that depends on the boss for instructions, clarification, information, decisions, motivation, and approval. Employees at lower levels, team members, or family members should know their relative importance in the overall undertaking. If these people suffer from low self-esteem or ignorance of what's going on, managers, team leaders, or heads of families will suffer from lack of adequate support.

Some Pitfalls for Team Leaders

Frequently, if the leaders aren't in close touch with the other team members, they think they are making excellent use of their own time when in reality they are causing havoc at lower levels. For example, a leader who fails to supply team members with as much information as they need to complete a project may jeopardize top-priority work. Or, by demanding action on a pet project, a leader may divert critical effort from the team's major objectives. (It's easy to picture this happening in a family in which the father or mother pursues a particular interest that may blind him or her to the requirements of the family as a unit.) Ironically, the pet project often turns out to be of very minor importance compared with the major work that suffered as a result of the interruption.

These pitfalls demonstrate the need for the implementation of a time-management program. Participation by the team leader or the head (or heads) of a family is of prime importance to the success of the program. Your family or team members will rightly resist if you impose on them a regimen in which you are unwilling to share. Imagine the thoughts of employees whose boss arranges a time-management seminar but doesn't participate in it. They will often legitimately observe, "The one who needs it most isn't here!" Time management must involve the whole team.

THE TIME-WASTER PROFILE

One effective way to launch a program of time management for the team is through a seminar on the subject conducted by a knowledgeable professional. Such a person will have no prejudices regarding individual personalities in the group. However, a manager and team can begin by developing a team profile of time wasters to obtain a needs analysis.* This profile will provide insight into the group's major time concerns provided all members, including the leader, participate in completing it.

Results of the profile should be validated with time logs; this procedure often reveals time-use problems of which we are unaware. Useful time-log exercises are available from various sources.† Perception of our actual time-use problems frequently changes dramatically after the logs are analyzed. If possible, the leader should be the first person to take a time log; this tends to remove the fear of its possible use as a surveillance tool. If the boss shares what has been learned with the team, this will further reduce uneasiness about the log's use and will encourage team members to see it as a self-

---

* Exercises in developing a team profile are included in "MEMO 2," which is available from Alec Mackenzie & Associates, P.O. Box 130, Greenwich, NY 12834; phone: 518-692-9626.

† For example, "MEMO 1" identifies human and managerial time barriers and solutions; "MEMO 2" identifies environmental and team time barriers and solutions and includes exercises in developing a team profile of time wasters. Both are available from Alec Mackenzie & Associates, P.O. Box 130, Greenwich, NY 12834; phone: 518-692-9626.

help tool. When employees are ordered, without explanation, to take time logs, there will probably be fear, apprehension, and resentment. In such situations the results are likely to be quite unsatisfactory.

A request by the leader for candid reactions to the profile and logs of the team as a whole and for suggestions in implementing change almost guarantees cooperation and success. The boss's shortcomings must be included in the action plan to gain the support of others in initiating change.

Once the team's time barriers have been confirmed, solutions to the top five should be developed jointly and actions to be taken should be agreed on by the team. Here again, in a less formal way, family members might agree to work on the items that dominate their shared lists.

Innovative Approaches

Your team may discover that solutions to its top time-use problems involve far too many actions to implement at once. An appealing and forceful recommendation is the "a change a week" plan, beginning with the most urgent time barrier of the group. Every manager will participate in deciding what action should be taken so that mutual reinforcement is generated. Throughout the week, when one manager may momentarily lapse into an old bad habit, associates will remind that person of the agreement or intention to act otherwise. Time-management implementation opens a new dimension in communication among staff members, and the role of well-placed humor as a motivator should not be overlooked.

Everyone enjoys the sense that they are learning on the job. A good way to provide this incentive within your department, group, or family is to institute a continuing study of some subject applicable to the team project. Such a subject may well be time management, and a stimulating experience would be to read a book about it with your team.

An exercise at the Aberdeen Proving Ground utilized *The Time Trap*. All team members were given copies of the book and assigned a chapter to read each week. A different member reported on each chapter, presenting recommendations that were discussed and either implemented or rejected. The supervisor told me that the results exceeded his highest expectations, principally because the effort was sustained and the suggestions came from the team.

Staff Meetings. Since reinforcement is crucial to success, I recommend that, initially, time management be placed on the agenda of every staff meeting for several months; thereafter it should be a topic at one meeting each month. The inclusion serves as an excellent reminder of the importance of the subject and should provide a measure of periodic progress. The team should discuss what *progress* has been made, what *problems* have arisen, and what the *plans* are for further improvement in their time-management practices.

The Buddy System. Interest in time management can be sustained by organizing a buddy system in which two or more managers agree to meet regularly to discuss their progress. They check on each other's performance and give suggestions to one another for implementation and reinforcement. Obviously, managers will select those with whom they are friendly, so communication will be candid and stimulating. This form of "going public" will help each manager avoid slipping back into undesirable habits. The buddy system was a most effective method for a group of schoolteachers and administrators with whom I worked in Canada.

Respect for Time = Increased Productivity

When time management is practiced by a team, a new sensitivity to the value of time as a resource pervades the group's daily activities. No longer do you hear "Got a minute?" unless the person requesting another's time has weighed the necessity of interruption. Employees begin to anticipate, rather than react, so that problems often can be prevented, rather than solved. A new respect for the time of others becomes apparent, and the productivity of the entire team rises.

One of the most beneficial results of managing time effectively as a team is the ability to estimate realistically time requirements for projects. This means that the scheduling of joint tasks becomes easier and the frustration of waiting for information from another person or department is removed. Deadlines no longer are selected casually but are developed carefully with adequate time provided to do the task right.

MANAGING TIME AT THE BOTTOM

Wait a minute! What about me? I'm not part of a team at work. I have no one below me to delegate to. My boss determines my priorities, and I just get on with the job. What can I get out of time management? This question is one I'm often asked, and you'll be glad to hear that there are interesting solutions. One young manager told me that she cut in half the amount of time formerly required to do her work by setting daily objectives, assigning priorities to the tasks necessary to achieve those objectives, and tenaciously working on a task until it was completed. She accomplished the last by sharing her priority list with her boss, which eliminated his previous habit of constantly shifting her priorities. And this manager was a person who answered her own phone and handled visitors to her office. No one reported directly to her. She learned that many of her interruptions were self-inflicted. Most of us are interruption-prone, finding it easy to interrupt or delay work on a project.

The person who works without assistance also can delegate

upward or laterally to others by persuasion. Sometimes the boss is working on a lower-priority task and may willingly accept responsibility for handling his or her own interruptions while a top-priority task is completed. Salespeople, engineers, and others who may have little or no secretarial help often can delegate responsibility for handling phone calls and visitors to each other on a rotating basis so that everyone is able to have an hour or two to concentrate without interruptions.

If you are hesitant to take such action, ask yourself who answers your phone when you are out to lunch or away from the office. No client or customer really expects that you will be available for phone calls every minute of the day. But whoever takes messages should be able to tell callers the expected time of your return and should ask if that would be a convenient time for a callback. In addition, the person should determine the purpose of each call, so that you will be better prepared when you return calls.

MANAGING TIME WITH YOUR BOSS

Most managers complain, "The boss doesn't have enough time for me" and "My subordinates take too much of my time." They are probably right on both accounts, Peter Drucker writes in his excellent article "How to Manage Your Boss."* Since our time with the boss is limited, we must learn to use it effectively. A summary of Drucker's ideas should help:

1. Determine whether your boss is a listener or a reader. If your boss is a reader, obviously you should present requests and ideas on paper first and talk afterward. The reverse will be true if your boss is a listener. Even then, preparation is necessary so that you will be ar-

---

*Peter Drucker, "How to Manage Your Boss," *Management Review*, May 1977.

ticulate and succinct in presenting your ideas. Do your homework and remember to follow up on discussions.

2. Remember that your boss is not a mind reader. Make sure your boss knows what you are trying to do now, what you will defer until later, and what decisions you have made.

3. If you have made a mistake or have a problem, don't hide it. Get it on the table while corrective action is still possible. Never attempt to hide an elephant.

4. While you shouldn't monopolize your boss's time, you are entitled to required advice. Request it, and use it sparingly.

5. Remember that your boss is a human being, an individual, and that it is better to overrate than to underrate the person for whom you work.

6. If all else fails, know when to abandon ship.

MANAGING TIME WITH YOUR SECRETARY OR ASSISTANT

The importance of recognizing the secretary or assistant as a full member of the management team is unquestioned by those who have worked with a professional assistant.* Inadequate, untrained support staff will damage the effectiveness of a management team. The role of the assistant on the management team is often misunderstood. Frequently, this person works for both a top manager and members on the team. An effective assistant serves as an ally to team members

---

*In this section, for readability, the terms "secretary" and "assistant" are used interchangeably.

in terms of facilitating requests for information and decisions. In acting as a liaison for the boss, the secretary will follow through and check progress on team projects. This may mean that team members will, at times, communicate with the boss indirectly through the secretary.

A middle-level manager once asked me resentfully: "Why must I communicate through the secretary? I make three times as much as she does." He felt rebuffed by his boss and, consequently, less important. Somehow his boss had failed to communicate to him the reason for this procedure. Perhaps it was a new practice in that office, only recently implemented and never clearly explained to anyone. If this was the case, such misunderstandings could be expected to recur. Or perhaps the young manager was new to the department and unfamiliar with this procedure. Either way, it is the boss's responsibility to clarify the channels of communication used in the department.

Working with Your Secretary and Other Support Staff

With today's technology, a manager can handle many tasks that were formerly done by a secretary or an assistant. For example, it's easy to access the contents of a computer file. However, typing skill is still necessary for inputting data or for sending electronic communications. Electronic files must be periodically cleaned out, phones answered, visitors handled, meetings arranged. Any manager with a heavy load of responsibility must rely on support staff to handle details.

While members of the support staff must be available and trained to handle details, they are only half the solution. Managers must know what to delegate and how to do so.

In a manager-secretary team relationship it is, obviously, the manager who will determine priorities, do only those tasks that cannot be delegated, and make major decisions. Of course, this does not mean that the assistant sits passively by. Managers who have worked with a professional secretary or assistant agree that he or she should take initiative, suggest priorities, screen out unnecessary interruptions without offending others, always maintain confidentiality, and, when needed, diplomatically question the boss's instructions.

Keeping Your Secretary Informed

Secretaries and administrative assistants need time with their bosses to be better informed, to get answers to their questions, and to clear the air if there are problems. If both manager and secretary are well organized, ten to fifteen minutes a day should suffice. Use the time to determine priorities, go over schedules, delegate routine matters, and obtain background information or materials that you will need during the day to accomplish priorities. You will find that interruptions of each other during the day are minimal if you adhere to a daily scheduled meeting.

When you undertake new projects, give your assistant relevant background information so that he or she will be able to answer questions and handle minor problems in your absence. When you leave the office, tell your assistant where you are going and the approximate time of your return. This prevents potential embarrassment when she or he is asked your whereabouts or planned return. Few will believe you left without saying, for example, "I'll be back at two thirty." Always enhance the credibility of your secretary or assistant by providing complete background information and all necessary instructions whenever you depart from the office.

The Secretary's Responsibility and Authority

Take time to develop a philosophy of how you and your secretary or assistant will work together and to determine what authority he or she should have, particularly when you are absent and when the assistant is dealing with managers who report to you. Once agreement has been reached, a job description for the secretary should be developed. Taking such action will eliminate misunderstandings and give the secretary the necessary backup required to do the job. Make your assistant's authority clear to your team members, their subordinates, and your boss.

In summary, the contacts necessary to ensure a smooth manager-secretary relationship should take place as follows:

1. daily (ten to fifteen minutes), to keep informed on day-to-day matters

2. routinely and briefly whenever boss leaves office

3. at start of any new project

4. rarely, but importantly, to establish philosophy of relationship and job description

5. periodically, at least quarterly, to discuss how the job is going and how well original expectations are being met

CASE STUDY 1

Most managers today share a secretary or an assistant. In a *Fortune* 500 corporation in White Plains, New York, where I conducted seminars over a period of years, a team of twelve managers shared one secretary. Jean, the secretary, suffered from poor motivation and frustration as all twelve managers brought her work to be typed, sent her on countless trips to the copy machine each day, and were themselves in a state of anxiety, wondering if their priority work would get typed in time to meet deadlines.

Jean and Mike, the head of the team, attended a time-management seminar along with eleven other manager-secretary teams from the division. They met to determine what action they could take to resolve particular problems facing their unit.

They discovered that Jean was spending her day typing documents in the order they were handed to her and running back and forth to the copy machine. In her particular case, an important time saver was eliminating unnecessary typing; for example, top management agreed that complete charts need not be typed—typing only the comments relating to the charts would be sufficient. The first lesson for the team was that every action should be questioned: "Is this task really necessary?"

Since a heavy load of typing still remained, the next step was to set priorities on all typing. Lesson number two for the team: Ensure that the most crucial work gets done by setting priorities for the unit. Jean still was unable to complete all the typing every day, but the most important work was accomplished and what was left over would not result in a crisis. If a conflict occurred on priorities, Mike, not Jean, would resolve it.

To accommodate Jean's schedule, managers agreed to do their own copying. Not only did this give Jean time to complete priorities, but it resulted in a sharp decrease in the amount of copying being done. Managers began to question whether a copy was really necessary. Another way of handling this would have been to consolidate copying, with Jean going to the machine only once or twice a day. Few matters are so urgent that they cannot wait an hour or two.

Jean became more involved with administrative details. She screened calls and visitors for an hour each day, giving Mike a quiet hour. Since the quiet hour was observed divisionwide, there were few interruptions, even for Jean. As meetings were a problem for Mike, Jean began to ask if his presence was necessary or if he could send someone in his place. This eliminated a number of meetings for Mike each week. For meetings initiated by Mike, Jean determined the purpose and organized an agenda and approximate time frame. She recorded minutes of the meetings so that everyone present fully understood what had been decided and who was responsible for follow-up.

Mike told me that his own effectiveness increased by 30 percent with this additional support from Jean and that no one in the department suffered. In fact, Mike said that, for the first time, managers recognized the value of time and were aware of the fact that the secretary's time was not "elastic"—it would not stretch indefinitely.

CASE STUDY 2

Molly Prior and her husband run a small family farm and are the parents of two teenage boys. Her husband is frequently away from home on business, so the day-to-day management of animals as well as household chores falls to Molly. As they live 12 miles from town, trips for school activities and shopping entail long drives. Besides looking after the home, Molly writes magazine articles and short stories and is very active in a local political group concerned with protecting the environment in their rural county.

When she began to be deeply involved in politics, Molly grew increasingly distraught. The house, always inconvenient and hard to keep clean, became a total mess. Beds were unmade, washing piled up, and clothes were never ready when needed. The garden was choked with weeds, the sheep went unshorn, the children rebelled against their mother's apparent withdrawal of attention, and Molly's husband felt put upon and resentful of his wife's outside interests. Molly stopped writing to her parents back home in Ireland.

One evening, one of her husband's clients showed them

how he used Time Tactics in his business operation. Molly warily began to apply it to her own situation. Not being a woman to do things by halves, she cleared her desk by turning it upside down! Then she ripped all the wisps of paper from the bulletin board and refrigerator and sat down at the empty desk with Time Tactics and a big wastebasket. She transferred all the phone numbers and important dates into the appropriate sections. Then she drew a deep breath of relief, took a walk around the house and garden, and came back in to write up her time log, priority list, and monthly plan.

Meetings, phone calls, and frequent long drives showed up on her log as constant consumers of her most valuable resource. With her monthly plan before her she began to reserve time for her necessary personal tasks and activities with the family. She was able to consolidate her trips to town and to set aside certain hours in the day for writing. She scheduled correspondence as a priority to be completed by the end of each weekend.

Now Molly consciously enjoys being in control of her life again. She is just as devoted to her political cause as ever, but it no longer dominates her every moment. The children are better at getting themselves out of the house every morning, since their room is efficiently organized so that they can find and choose appropriate clothes without yelling for help. They are not sure why home seems a better place to come back to after school, but Molly knows each time she catches sight of her empty desktop and the week's letter to Ireland addressed and ready to go.

A TIMELY FUTURE

What I am proposing then, is that to use time efficiently, we must become more objective-oriented and less process-oriented. Until you've established your goals, much of your activity is pointless. You have to answer the question "Why?"

before you can take up the question of *how* something can be accomplished. Activity-prone people tend to be impatient with theory. This is a mistake, because when conditions change, those who failed to understand the "why" of their actions will not be able to adapt their actions to the new circumstances. Accordingly, we need to devote some time to reflection—taking stock of where we are headed, why we want to get there, and whether or not we have chosen the best route. Don't be afraid to be caught at your desk or in your study just thinking.

Remember: Success means doing your best. As a successful person, you will be goal-oriented. You will make it a habit to set goals that are measurable and attainable, yet challenging. Your goals will also be deadlined, participative, consistent, and written. You know that without time you will never achieve your goals, so you will focus on effective time control in order to break your human, managerial, and environmental time barriers. Time is on your side—the moment you organize it.

With goals and time, success can be yours.

APPENDIX:
TIME TACTICS

There are many organizing systems which, when used alone, will have no more practical effect than the simplest diary or to-do list. Some diaries give us an easy way to schedule dates or record things we need to do; others also keep track of names, addresses, or personal information. None gives us a comprehensive planning and tracking mechanism for getting and staying organized.

The to-do list in isolation may pose even more serious problems because it gives the user the illusion of being organized. The list has a number of defects, however. In most cases it provides no priority review mechanism, no tracking of delegated tasks, no calendaring of deadlines, no automatic follow-up after task completion, no task allocation across available time, no information retrieval as needed, and no preservation of completed lists.

When developing or choosing an organizing system, it is vital to realize that all the tools and techniques in the world will not keep a person organized without a method of integrating these tools—a system that makes them easy to use and provides a built-in reinforcement mechanism to keep the system working.

One such system is Time Tactics.* Its elements include modules for:

daily-weekly plans

monthly plans

objectives

projects

contacts

alphabetical directory

Using this system, you no longer need to have several notebooks available at all times, or rely on "reminders" jotted down on separate little bits of paper. Everything you have to do or remember can go into the Time Tactics organizer. You can track your long-range objectives to the day of execution, and you can keep a record of decisions made along the way. Notes from discussions with key people, along with deadlines, can be entered in a special contact log with an identifying tab. If any items require immediate attention, they can be noted under today's action items in the weekly plan section. It is an overall system that works to ensure that everything you must do is brought to your attention when, where, and how you need it.

Time Tactics gives you a way to easily scan your goals and projects. There are places for planning your day, your week, and your month, and space for you to record key decisions, together with the names of important contacts for instant retrievability. This simple system provides a goal list, an ap-

---

*Time Tactics is a planner-organizer available from Alec Mackenzie & Associates, P.O. Box 130, Greenwich, New York, 12834; phone: 518-692-9626.

pointment schedule, and a to-do list for each day, as well as weekly and monthly planning sections, objectives and projects sections, a contact log, and an alphabetical directory of key names, phone numbers, and addresses.

These elements are coordinated so that it is easy to transfer a task that needs to be done today from one of the "back burner" lists. Such an item could be something you may have jotted down only the previous afternoon or something that came to your attention a month or so ago and now needs to be done: an appointment to be kept at a certain hour or a task to be worked into the day whenever possible. Time Tactics also provides a place to note follow-up actions with suppliers or other contacts. Entries on the contact log keep the manager up to date on the present situation. Entries in the calendar section can keep checkpoints from slipping by unnoticed. When information is required, it is on hand.

The weekly plan is the focus of the system because it governs your activities on any given day. You can see the entire week at a glance. For detailed planning, you can carry with you as many weeks in advance as is practical, because Time Tactics is a loose-leaf system. There's no need to copy a note two or three times, as often happens when you rely entirely on a typical to-do list. There is a place to list goals for each day, which will induce you to concentrate on the most important matters. While everything may not get done, this makes it much more likely that the highest priorities will be accomplished and that what doesn't get done will be the least important. Further, by seeing the week at a glance, you can clearly see when you have scheduled a full day.

The monthly plan section provides eighteen monthly calendars, taking you to June of the following year. In this section you can list all set dates for the year: birthdays, business, and personal. It provides the means, not only for ample advance planning, but also for reminders of follow-ups, checkpoints, and fixed events. As the dates become current, they can be transferred to the weekly plan section. When the previous four weeks are removed to the permanent file marked "Weekly Plan," the current four weeks are added to the Time Tactics manual. The monthly section provides instant reference for long-range planning. There is a purposely small to-do section for every day, because there are always a few actions you wish to remind yourself of daily that can't be scheduled. With Time Tactics such unscheduled, and therefore frequently unfinished, "to do's" eventually disappear. All you must do is schedule every task for completion as a "goal."

It is generally agreed that the two most common reasons for the failure of management by objectives are (1) losing sight of the objectives, and (2) not breaking them down into manageable segments. Time Tactics solves both problems. The objectives and projects sections provide places for listing key-result targets and supporting goals, as well as start and finish dates and progress checkpoints. The contact log contains an agenda section for items to be discussed and important decisions to be made with key contacts. A separate tab is provided for each person with whom you deal on a regular basis. Not only does this ensure that important matters will not be overlooked when the time for discussion arrives, it also makes needed information instantly available. The contact log greatly reduces in-house interruptions and memos. You can jot down questions, facts, and answers and will be able to retrieve them whenever they are needed.

Of course, no system will work if you don't pay attention to it. The real key to effective use of Time Tactics is scheduling time at the end of each day to review your day's accomplishments and to update those tasks not completed. You should do the same at the end of each week and the end of each month.

Time Tactics, the most practical time management system ever devised, increases productivity, reduces stress, and puts you in control of your job and your life.

INDEX